Auto Repossession Business Success

Brad Shrader

© 2018 by Brad Shrader

ISBN 978-1-7325700-0-9

DISCLAIMER: The author nor any of his companies make any representations or warranties of any kind with respect to the legality and sufficiency of the information in the book. The book content may not reflect the most current legal developments, verdicts, settlements, or opinions and should not be considered an indication of future results. Any websites, URL's, apps, services, or products listed are not endorsements, rather suggestions to the reader as options. These websites, apps, services, or products may change their services or fees or may not be in business in the future, and the author has no control over or involvement in those decisions.

This book is not offered as, nor can it be construed to be, legal advice. Therefore, readers should obtain the advice of competent counsel in reference to starting, owning, or operating a repossession company. The examples contained in the book are for illustrative purposes only.

DEDICATION

I would like to dedicate this book to my wife, Punnawit. If every man had a wife just like you, the world would be overflowing with success stories!

Thank you for believing in me and encouraging me to be a better man every day. You always make me feel unstoppable, confident, and capable of doing anything I set my mind to do. When I read Proverbs 31:10-31, I see you in every single verse! You are the virtuous wife. I love you!

ACKNOWLEDGMENTS

IT WOULD BE impossible for me to thank everyone in my life's journey who made this book possible.

First of all, I would like to thank Tom Hudson of the Hudson and Cook law firm for not only encouraging me to write this book, but for also taking time out of his busy schedule to mentor me in so many ways.

I would also like to thank my first boss, friend and business mentor, Bill Colfax. Without you, I would not be the man I am today in both my personal and professional life.

I would also like to thank my pastor, Arlyn Walters, for his never-wavering friendship, support and love.

I would like to thank my son Brandon for being a young man who has taught an older man so much about life. More importantly, he helped me to learn how to live that life to its fullest. Son, you are wise beyond your years!

Most of all, I would like to thank my God for never giving up on me and for showing me immeasurable grace throughout my years.

Hundreds of other friends, family members, and mentors have influenced me in so many ways that have contributed to the writing of this book. I thank all of you.

ABOUT THE AUTHOR

Brad "The Bulldog" Shrader has spent nearly a quarter of a century working in the auto repossession industry. His work experience ranges from being a storage lot worker, an account specialist, a repossession agent, a skip tracer, a transporter, an auto repossession company manager and trainer, and a consultant for creditors, forwarders, auto repossession company owners, and agents across the nation.

Besides owning a skip tracing and private investigative firm, he was also the owner of a very successful and profitable auto repossession company that had a fleet of trucks and multiple office locations. He has been a consultant in the auto repossession industry, the COO of a publicly traded company, a restaurant owner, a real estate investor, an Internet entrepreneur, and the owner of several small businesses.

He owns *repoindustry.com*, a website where repossession company owners, agents, and clients can network and where there is a discussion forum and state directory where repossession company owners can advertise their companies.

TABLE OF CONTENTS

I Want to Own a Repossession Company

As long as I can remember, I have never desired to be a "worker bee," spending my days punching a clock and answering to "the man." While all the other kids were out playing basketball and kick the can, I wanted to set up a lemonade stand, wash cars in my driveway, mow lawns in the neighborhood, or start some other small business. Those early ideas and ventures did not yield a lot of money, but they were my ideas, my hard work, and all me. They were mine, and I answered to no one!

I had a paper route when I was a kid, and although I enjoyed getting paid to ride my bike and throwing my newspapers, I started wondering how I could be the owner of my own newspaper. I got a friend involved, and we started pecking out a weekly newspaper on a manual typewriter I found on a shelf in my parents' basement. We went around the neighborhood, knocking on doors and trying to sell copies for a nickel.

Learning From a Mentor

I believe that newspaper idea was where I came up with the thought to work for someone, figure out how to operate that particular business, determine whether or not it was run well and how it could be run better. When I was 15, I took a job flipping burgers at a local American diner in my hometown. While I was flipping burgers on the grill and tossing frozen fries in the deep fryer, I was also watching the manager and the boss handle customers, check inventory, order product, and manage the restaurant staff. After analyzing that business for about four months, I had developed a plan for exactly how I would own and operate my own diner and better manage the establishment. I never forgot what I had learned and what twist I would add to mine. Twenty-three years later, I owned my own American diner!

I graduated from high school at the age of 17, and soon afterward I moved out of my parents' house to a rented one-bedroom apartment on the north side of Chicago. My $300 rent seemed super-expensive at the time. A few years ago I checked on the fee for renting that same apartment and found the going price was over $2000 a month. I came to know the landlord of that apartment building, and he became my first mentor for my future endeavor of real-estate investing. He answered my numerous questions, teaching me valuable lessons about that industry.

I got to know the owner of an auto body paint and supply company located right outside my apartment door. Bill asked me to come work for him in a not-so-glamorous position as a delivery driver. I looked up to Bill and enjoyed being around him, so I happily accepted the job. Bill was not only a great boss, but he became a mentor and a personal friend for life. Working for Bill was probably one of the main reasons why I continued my quest of being "time-clock free"! He taught me more about business, personal relationships, personal finance, integrity, and life than any other mentor I have ever had.

Besides Bill's being a life-changing mentor, I also learned from him everything about the auto body paint and supply business. I analyzed his business thoroughly, noted what he was doing well and came up with some ideas that I felt would better benefit the company. People would call in and order supplies, the store staff would box them up, write up a bill, hand it all to me, and I would deliver it to the body shop placing the order. Once the appropriate person signed the ticket, the shop had thirty days to pay. Most of those customers paid the bill on time, but several did not.

I felt that I could help Bill's business by upselling for him. I carried many products in my vehicle that I knew body shops used daily. While I was making a delivery, I would also check to see if they needed anything like body filler, dust masks, tape, tack cloth, fisheye killer, paint thinner, sanding disks, and a myriad of other supplies. Every body shop generally bought multiple items, but I had them pay cash. A couple of shop owners even called Bill because they thought I might be stealing from him and selling his inventory for fast cash! Bill assured them that was not my intention, and he loved the extra profit I was bringing in every day from my upsell efforts.

Eventually, I asked Bill if I could start my own auto body supply business outside of his local area. I did not want to mix and sell paint for cars, only everyday supplies. I asked him to buy the product in bulk from his vendors and offered him a cut of the sales. Before it was over, my business was up and running and growing by leaps and bounds.

Why am I sharing these stories that are unrelated to the auto repossession industry? Because being a business owner is not simply something you flippantly decide to do on a whim. You have to want it with all of your being. You have to commit to it and decide that owning a business is what you are going to do even if you have to suffer at first. You have to be willing to sacrifice, to be confident, to be willing to give it everything you have—even when things seem hopeless.

Do You Really Want It?

Before you read any further in this book, you need to ask yourself this question, "Do I really want to be a business owner, or do I feel more comfortable punching a clock and collecting a guaranteed check?" You also need to ask yourself, "Why do I want to be a business owner?"

From experience I can assure you that working for yourself can be an emotional and economical roller coaster. Not only do you have to invest a great deal of money in a startup that may or may not work, but there is also the great investment of time in the long hours spent running a business. You not only have to worry about taking care of yourself and your family, but you also have to worry about taking care of any employees that you may have and their families as well. If you fail at your auto repossession business, you fail them too. You may be willing to work for free when money is short, but your employees will probably not have the same dedication to your business endeavor that you do. Are you ready for all of the stress and worry that comes with being a business owner?

The good news is that although owning a business has its dreaded valleys, it also has its mountaintops. There is the joy of success that owning a business brings. There is the satisfaction in being a contributing member to one's community and the local economy. There is certainly pride in ownership of a business and the great feeling of knowing that you are your own boss.

Some other questions you also need to ask yourself about wanting to own an auto repossession company include the following:

- Is it because you watched some overly dramatic, staged reality television show about auto repossessions?

- Is it because you think you are a "tough guy" that can bully people into turning over their cars?

- Are you a "tough guy" that likes confrontations?

If any of these reasons are why you are interested in this profession, then you need put down this book and look for other career options.

The truth is that a professional repossession agent rarely experiences confrontation because he knows how to talk to people to calm them down as soon as the situation starts to get out of hand. A successful repossession agent is not a "tough guy" who enjoys confrontation, but a quiet professional who secures his client's collateral without any drama. He is neither a bully nor a fighter, but more of a compassionate and understanding person. He realizes people sometimes get down on their luck and still deserve to be treated with respect. He always conducts himself professionally and knows that he is not only a repossession agent, but also a business owner in the community in which he resides. Therefore, he should conduct himself accordingly at all times.

So what is a good reason for owning a repossession company? I believe if it is operated correctly, an auto repossession business is one of the last, few small businesses the average person can still afford to own in this day and age. Some people may find the phrase "Mom-and-Pop" business offensive, but in the repossession industry, more than likely, that is exactly what it is. However, auto repossession is a "Mom-and-Pop" business that does work for multi-million dollar nationwide auto lenders and finance companies. This business can grow from a family business to employing dozens of staff if operated correctly. This business has potential, and as long as people are financing cars, there will always be a need for someone to execute repossessions when the debt is not being paid. This business can support a family quite well and also be passed down to descendants when the owner is ready to retire.

A word of caution: before you run out to form a corporation and buy a wrecker, be sure that you are ready to be a repossession company owner. It would be very foolish to do so without any experience in the auto repossession industry. Countless people start auto repossession businesses with no experience, and most of them do not even last a year. These individuals invested an abundance of money in a business about which they knew nothing, and most of them went broke.

This is not to say that a veteran repossession agent is guaranteed success in this industry, because that is not the case either. Many top-notch repossession agents have started their own repo business and failed. They were great repo agents, but not good at business. They could find all sorts of collateral, but they were not good with business skills such as sales, accounting, and management. Being a business owner requires a combination of being a good businessman, a skip tracer, a repossession agent, a marketer, a manager, and a whole lot of other qualities that are required to make it in this industry.

So if you are somewhat of a businessman, then you need to get your repo skills up to par. You should work for a reputable repossession company for a few years at the very least and probably several years before opening your own repossession business. No repossession is ever the same, and no matter how much experience you have, you will often find yourself in a unique situation, wondering how to deal with it. Oftentimes, you need to make a snap decision that could keep you or someone else from being injured or killed.

Not only should you work in the field as a repossession agent, but you should also perform and learn all of the other staff positions that are necessary to make a repo company run like a finely tuned machine. These positions include being a spotter, a storage lot worker, a locksmith, a skip tracer, an account representative, a repossession company manager, a salesman, an auction transporter, and maybe even the company janitor.

You cannot learn only one of those jobs if you want to be a successful business owner. They all fit perfectly together to make a repossession company run smoothly. This will be needed when you need to train new employees or fill in when someone is out to lunch or ill. You also need to know the entire operation of the company down to each job description when selling your company to a potential client.

However, if you do decide to open your own company, do not use your employment as an opportunity to steal clients from your boss. If you learn to be a great repo agent, clients will hear you opened your own company and follow you wherever you go. Another option is that your boss may eventually want to sell his repossession company, and this possibility may be an even better option than launching your own company from the ground up. Purchasing a company that you work for can bring you instant revenues through its existing client base. It will also help in growing the client base if the company has a good reputation. In order to have a smooth transition and not lose these existing clients, you will want to be sure the purchase is set up correctly. You may also have to keep the owner as a partner with no control over the company. This can be done by keeping his shares very low with a buyout clause for a set amount after a set time.

Again, I truly believe that an auto repossession business is one of the last "Mom-and-Pop" American dream businesses that the average, blue-collar American can afford to start in today's America. I have always had a great love for this industry and have truly enjoyed every minute of helping others reach their dream of owning an auto repossession business and being greatly successful at doing so.

HAVE PLANS AND GOALS

A Business Plan

Nearly every other week, I am approached by someone about partnering on some sort of business venture or another. In fact, right before I began typing this chapter, I was visited by a very successful educator who wanted me to finance her in opening a private school for children with learning disabilities. Although I am sure the need exists for such a business and it might even be highly profitable, I halted the conversation rather quickly.

When I asked her what was unique about the company, she had no real answer. I asked if the business had a high growth potential. She did not know. She told me that she had some interesting ways to teach children with learning disabilities, so I asked if she had a sample of the curriculum with her. She pointed at her temple and told me the curriculum was in her head. After that third question, I ended the discussion. She had no written plan to present to me nor a detailed list of goals.

Why is it that some people succeed in life and business and others continually struggle or even fall flat on their face? **A plan!** If you ask anyone who knows me, I am famous for quoting John "Hannibal" Smith from *A-Team* fame when I achieve something that I am trying to do: "I love it when a plan comes together!"

I will not go into detail on how to write a business plan for an auto repossession business. Plenty of boiler-plate business plan templates already exist that you can utilize. I also know of at least one auto repossession business plan online for sale. Put in the time and write your own comprehensive business plan. If you do not do that, buy a business plan or pay someone to write one for you. Having a business plan does not always guarantee success, but not having one can almost always guarantee failure. And if having no plan does not spell failure, the likelihood is that the business will be a much less successful venture than it could have been.

If you are going to be a successful repossession company owner, you must have a detailed, sensible plan to get you from point A to point B. There is good news! The next several paragraphs are going to help you in establishing this plan and more! The "more" is because I care about you more than just in the area of the auto repossession industry, so I will teach you how to set some personal goals for life as well. I will also try to teach you how to have a healthy and successful mindset.

Simply purchasing this book means that you are wanting to change your life and become a businessman. Now it is time to make a planned commitment towards your success.

Put It on Paper!

Your goals need to be put down on paper and reviewed daily. Tape a piece of paper on your bathroom mirror that says, "Review Your Goals Now!" Set an alert on your smart phone that notifies you several times a day to review your goals. Carry your list of goals with you everywhere you go. Share your list of goals with your spouse, a family member, or a close friend and ask them to remind you often to stay on top of your goals.

Make sure the person with whom you share them is not a negative person who will downplay your goals. Only share them with someone who will encourage you to succeed!

Make sure your goals are quantifiable so you have a way to track your goals. Setting a goal to own a bunch of towing equipment by the time you are in your mid-forties is not quantifiable. However, setting a goal to own 15 wreckers by the time you are 45 years old can easily be measured.

You may see the need to adjust your goals as time goes by too. For example, you may set a goal to own four wreckers, a roll back, a commercial office, and a storage lot by a certain date but find yourself below or even above that number.

Your Present Reality

Let's consider your present reality today:

- What is your current net worth?

- What is your monthly cash flow currently?

- What is your lifestyle like right now?

- How much happiness does your current situation provide you?

- Currently, how much time do you have to spend with your family and doing things you enjoy?

Your Desired Reality

Now, let's lay out what you want your desired reality to be like in the future:

- What would you like your net worth to be?

- Where would you like to see your monthly cash flow at?
- What type of lifestyle do you want to have?
- How much happiness would you like to experience?
- How much free time would you like to have?

Now make a list of the actions you need to take to move your situation from your present reality to your desired reality.

Make your first daily goal to review all of your goals from your list every single day. Set a goal on how much studying of this repossession industry you plan to do each day/week. Set a goal every week to research online information found in forums, blogs, and online classes that pertain to this industry, entrepreneurship, and owning a small business.

Make your daily and weekly goals somewhat auto repossession specific, but keep in mind that it does not hurt to add in ideas and specifics that will improve your life in other areas. These goals may also include reading blogs, articles, magazines, and books on success.

Detail some family goals you would like to make. Some ideas might be setting a weekly or biweekly date night or attending a certain number of your child's sporting and/or other school events, or maybe spending a set number of minutes a night helping your kids with their homework or playing with them. List any personal goals that you feel are important to you and your family.

The Importance of Healthy Living

There are lots of obese repo agents and company owners all

across America. Please, for your health's sake, list some fitness and diet goals. One could be joining a local gym and committing in writing to how many days a week you plan on working out. Consider making some written decisions on diet or calorie changes that you wish to make to become a healthier you. If you want to lose a half a pound a week, one pound, or more, then list that goal. You may be a person who wants to gain weight; list that weekly goal as well. Believe it or not, if your health and fitness is operating at an optimum level, your goals will be reached more easily. Your quality of life will also be greater when you are at your healthiest!

What good is achieving your dreams, success and financial independence if you are too unhealthy to enjoy the rewards of your labor?

Family-Centered Goals

Detail some family goals you would like to reach. Some ideas might be setting a weekly or biweekly date night with your soul mate.

Perhaps you will want to attend a certain number of your child's sporting events or other school activities, or maybe spending a set amount of time at night to help your kids with their homework or playing with them.

List any personal goals that you feel are important to you and your family. Remember, without your family and quality time spent with them, wealth and success are worthless!

First-Year Goals

Your first-year business goals need to be attainable ones. If you set goals that you cannot possibly reach, you will easily become discouraged and possibly give up on your plan.

As you attempt to achieve these goals, do not become discouraged if you do not always hit the mark. See this year of business goals as a football game. Most fans understand that several plays must be run to get the ball into the end zone. The quarterback and his running backs try to make as many first downs as they can as the team moves the ball down the field closer to the goal line. The quarterback might get sacked a few times as he tries to move the ball down the field. There may be some incomplete passes and even the occasional turnover as the game is played.

For the quarterback and his team to stay on the offensive is important. The businessman is the quarterback, and he must realize that not every play (aka *deal*) will turn out in his favor. Just like the quarterback does not score a touchdown every drive down the playing field, neither will the business owner. However, like the quarterback formulates a play that moves the ball into the end zone and scores a touchdown, the business owner will get a deal done—his touchdown, so to speak!

I use this football analogy because a 9:00 to 5:00 job is far different from being a real estate investor. When you are a business owner, a check is not always forthcoming after a 40-hour work week, nor will you get overtime and scheduled vacations. Often little victories, just like plays in football, move you down the field toward the end zone. You will eventually score in business, so be patient!

Your first-year goals should include how many wreckers

or other equipment you initially plan to buy. Goals might also include how much time you plan to spend on contacting potential clients to get work as well as how many sales calls you plan to make each week. It certainly should include a goal on how many involuntary and voluntary repossessions you want to do each month. A goal needs to be set regarding your need to grow a certain number of pickups each month and quarter as well. Without business growth, you won't make it in this business.

Whatever those goals might be, make sure you document them and commit to doing your best to achieve them. Again, keep these goals realistic, but more importantly have some!

One- to Eight-Year Goals

This goal list could include where you want your business to be in the next one to eight years. How many repossessions would you like to handle each year, starting for year 1 through year 8? Have a plan as to how you will increase that number year after year.

Your list might also include how much cash you would like to have in the bank and how much you want to add to it each year. This goal could be cash used for business growth and also personal monies you might save. Think about and note how much you would like to contribute to a retirement account and a college fund for your children each year.

Be Ready to Adjust

Be ready to adjust your goals to be less or more. I found myself reaching five out of six of my business goals in the middle of year two and had to make some uptick changes to this goal list. There is no right or wrong when it comes to listing your goals. You cannot fail by adjusting them, by adding more goals, or by taking some away. You do not get an "F" if you succeed at only 50 percent of your written goals. The only time you do not receive a passing grade is when you do not make a list at all!

Lifetime Goals

Your lifetime goals might include a finale of the successes you would like to attain in your lifetime. Perhaps your goal might be to own the largest repossession company in your state with revenues in the millions of dollars. Detail how much towing equipment you would like to own free and clear. Set a goal to own a commercial property for you company that is paid off. If your company is debt-free, then you can rest easy without worrying about making enough to cover operational costs in your later years. You can also have a plan in place to turn over a profitable, debt-free business to your children. Real success in business spans generations!

Giving Back

You should consider including charitable giving to your church, volunteering your time, and helping the needy and other charitable organizations. As you increase in blessings, increase the blessings that you pass on to others. Use your extra money for the greater good, as well as for improving your own life and your family's life.

Lifetime goals may include what you would like to do for your children and grandchildren in gifts, business, college funding, and more. This goal list may include major philanthropy projects, doing great things to help your church, and giving to the needy and other charitable organizations. You may attain such great success in your lifetime that you could consider setting up a foundation or scholarship fund. I know of an 85-year-old businessman who, in his lifetime, has reportedly given over $40 million dollars to churches and missionaries around the world. Could you be this man or woman in the future?

Unattainable Goals

This final list of goals you are about to make is a list of goals you feel you could never, ever attain. You may be asking yourself why this list is important. If you shoot for Mars, you may just land on the moon, or you might make it all the way to Mars. Set these goals high and work toward them. If you never make all of them or even one of them, you will still achieve greatness and success.

WHAT SHOULD BE ON
MY UNATTAINABLE GOALS LIST?

List goals that you are certain you will never, ever be able to achieve. You may be wondering why I am making this suggestion. Because you may reach a goal or two or more later on in life that today you cannot possibly imagine ever being reached!

I know of one repossession company owner who started

small but had aspirations he has said he never thought he would attain. He has grown his business over the years to operating in multiple states and US territories and owns millions of dollars worth of equipment and commercial real estate.

You never know where your venture will take you, so dream big! It will never hurt you, but most definitely will help you in some way or another. It is a great feeling when your dreams come true. It is an even bigger and better feeling when your big dreams come to fruition!

The following are some examples of what some people I know personally ended up owning that they never thought would be possible.

- **A Yacht.** I know one businessman who dreamed of owning a yacht but never expected to own one. But he always dreamed of the day that he might own one. He went to boat and yacht shows, read yacht magazines, and took pictures of yachts that he saw docked or on the water. Years later, he and his wife attended an auction with a yacht up for bid. He got in on the bidding process and was able to purchase that yacht he always dreamed of owning—for pennies on the dollar!

- **A Steelworker, a Farm, a Plane, and Flying.** I know several average people who have been able to afford to own planes as a result of good business practices. I knew a union steelworker who dreamed of living on a farm away from the city. He possessed a pilot's license and also dreamed of owning a small plane with the opportunity to fly as much as possible. He did not make much money but never stopped dreaming of a plane and a farm.

He ended up buying a farm at a tax sale over two hours from the steel mill where he worked. Soon after he bought the farm, a man approached him about buying a portion of his land. He sold some acreage at a huge profit and was able to purchase a small Cessna plane. His commute to work was now four hours a day, so he started flying to work every day and landing at a small airport near his workplace. He left a car at each airport so he could drive to work and home after he landed. He achieved three of his dreams—a farm, a plane, and flying every day! If a blue-collar steelworker can own a plane, the possibility of your possessing one can happen someday too!

■ **A Home on the Ocean.** An old Southern gentleman whom I know had always dreamed of living on beach-front property. He thought about having a boat docked at his house so he could go crabbing, fishing, and boating whenever he wanted to. He was a country boy who grew up in relative poverty, and no one expected him to do anything with his life. Well, that country boy went to college, and after he earned his degree, he was accepted into one of the most prominent law schools in America. After he obtained his law license, he ended up being a founding partner of an extremely successful law firm in a niche market. His law firm grew fast and brought on clients across the country. His firm eventually owned offices and employed lawyers all across America. He bought his house on the ocean with a boat docked right outside his door. In all actuality, he had many more things he never thought possible!

You should list anything and everything that you only dream about—what you are absolutely sure you will never have the possibility of owning! One day, when you have that unattainable dream, please get in touch with me and share that unbelievable story with me.

A Healthy Mindset

Finally, to be a successful auto repossession company owner or owner of any business for that matter, you must have the right kind of mindset. Wealthy business owners possess a highly developed, healthy mindset that allows them to realize their goals. They are incredibly optimistic and positive about their future. They know where they want to be in a year, five years, and longer, and they envision themselves being successful.

They don't ever allow negative outside influences to hinder their progress. They surround themselves with positive people and those who are cheerleader types who will help them reach their goals. In fact, if they have to, they will remove toxic and negative people from their lives.

If you have negative people in your life, do not ask them for advice. Do not share your hopes and dreams of owning an auto repossession business with them. If you do, plan on hearing how you won't succeed, that your idea is a dumb one, and other comments that will also discourage you.

Only discuss your plans with the positive people in your life. If you can, find a mentor or a business coach to help you along in your journey in becoming a business owner. You may not be able to afford to pay a coach or a mentor, but you might find a friend or a family members who will be in your corner, cheering you on!

CHAPTER TWO

What collateral recovery certifications
do your repossession agents have?
Or did Sonia P. train them?

THE TRUTH:
REALITY TV VS.
THE REPOSSESSION BUSINESS

W HEN I FIRST got into the auto repossession industry, it was kind of a secret club. The general public knew cars were routinely repossessed, but how the process worked and who handled the process was almost mysterious. In my eyes, the business was somewhat of a special fraternity or secret society.

Then one day I turned on the television and watched all sorts of drama, breach of peace, assaults, and downright silliness. I changed the channel and never watched another episode. But seemingly, every debtor and "wannabe" repo man was mesmerized by something that was not even close to what the real world of auto repossessions is all about. From the moment that the repo business hit the small screen, it seemed debtors started acting violently, and renegade "cheapo repo" companies operated by cowboys started popping up all over the place.

Everybody I met wanted a job working for me, and everyday I met someone at the filling station who said, "I used to repo." Seemingly half the population of my town had repossessed cars at one time or another in their life!

I used to hear that statement, and I would step into my wrecker and laugh my head off as I drove away.

As I said, I have only actually sat down one time and watched a reality TV show in its entirety. From that first viewing, it was obvious that the show was all Hollywood hype. Nothing I saw depicted what really happens with auto repossessions and the running of a legitimate repossession company.

I only watched a program one time; however, through the years, I have seen various brief clips and shots of the headlocks, the punching, the fist fighting, the wrestling on the ground, the blood, the cursing, and other definite breach-of-peace scenarios. I can tell you, from my extensive experience in the industry, no legitimate lender would be a part of an auto repossession reality show. Neither would they even consider contracting with a repo company where that type of silliness occurred even one time! The liability of such an endeavor would never pass the lender's due diligence "sniff test."

If what you see on a television show was really happening, I can assure you that debtors would form a line at the nearest law firm to collect on a sure-to-win lawsuit. What is demonstrated in these shows is definitely breach of peace. With all of the physical altercations portrayed in these shows, the agent and debtors would both be in jail facing all sorts of charges.

The television industry is well aware that sex, drama, and violence sell. The reality repo shows do not often resort to sex, but they are chock-full of drama and violence. Fighting and action drive the viewership on the repo shows. The people watching these shows are expecting to see acts of violence and all sorts of drama. These auto repossessions are undoubtedly staged and rehearsed. If the debtors on the show are real, they are contacted first, contracted second, and paid handsomely—probably enough to pay the balance due on their car loan. The scenes are definitely planned and probably rehearsed. You have to guess that the debtors are coached into putting on a show for the cameras and excited to get their 15 minutes of fame.

According to *Wikipedia.com*, the show *Lizard Lick Towing* is an improvised television show filmed in a style of film making known as Cinéma vérité. Wikipedia states that "this sort of *realism* was criticized for its deceptive pseudo-natural construction of reality." All of us know that these shows are deceptive in what is being depicted.

Without all of the antics, no one would be watching the auto repossession reality shows. The shows would be about as boring as the reality of owning an auto repossession business or working as a repossession agent. For the most part, owning or working for a repossession company is almost just that—one step above boring to make it a fun job.

Most repossessions are executed without a hiccup while the debtor is sound asleep in his bed. The majority of repossessions that involve debtor contact are never violent or even the least bit dramatic. And if they are, the skilled repo agent knows how to disarm and de-escalate volatile situations. Sure, when it comes to the auto repossession world, we can thank God that excitement and danger are not an everyday occurrence.

I always found the work to be enjoyable and challenging. No two days were ever the same. In fact, rarely were two repos ever the same. I found I was always learning something new, and I was able to see new things and meet new people every day.

The professional auto repossession company owners I know would never think to have their business and their day-to-day operations filmed for a reality repo show. They are quiet professionals who spend their evenings looking for collateral and their days returning property to debtors, transporting cars to auctions, balancing their books, and making sales calls. They would never want to be in the Hollywood limelight, rolling around on the ground with some guy dressed in a ninja outfit. In fact, they never brag to people that they are the "repo man" and rarely talk about their repossession job.

I have never met a repossession company owner or an agent who said that the repo shows seen on television represent the auto repossession industry. In fact, nearly everyone I talk to on this matter agrees that reality television hurts our industry. Most of the professionals I know feel that many people that watch the repo shows cannot separate reality from fiction and believe the show content to be true. They see debtors and repossession agents arguing, fighting, chasing each other at high speed, and more, and they think these sorts of actions are the norm. So when they find themselves up for repossession, they emulate what they saw on television and believe these actions to be acceptable.

The end result of this television-taught "learned repo experience" they are reliving is the injury or death of an agent, debtor, or bystander. This confrontation will be followed by someone's going to jail and another news story of an auto repossession "gone bad" splattered across the news and the Internet.

Legitimate repossession agents would like to ban repo shows from television. Of course, most of them know that this movement to ban them will never come to fruition. And why would it? Freedom of speech in America is the foundation on which our great country was built. The best to hope for is a loss in popularity of these types of shows, leading to their cancellation. Maybe in the future, the world can be further educated about the repossession industry with television documentaries that represent what truly professional repossession agents really do.

If you are thinking of launching your auto repossession career or starting a repossession business based on what you have seen on the repo reality shows, please put aside this book and seriously reconsider! You are not needed in this industry! Your erroneous perception will surely hurt the business and, more than likely, get you arrested, seriously injured, or even killed. Television is entertainment, and all of us enjoy getting wrapped up in a great show. But be sure you can separate the fact from the fiction. Many people are obsessed with the current series *The Walking Dead*, but no one wants to live in that mess.

Reality television should actually be called "unreality television" because the reality is actually owning and operating a repossession business in the real world—not something scripted that can be re-shot until the footage is approved by some file editing department. Reality will set in when you find yourself scrambling to keep your business running profitably and safely day after day, month after month, and year after year.

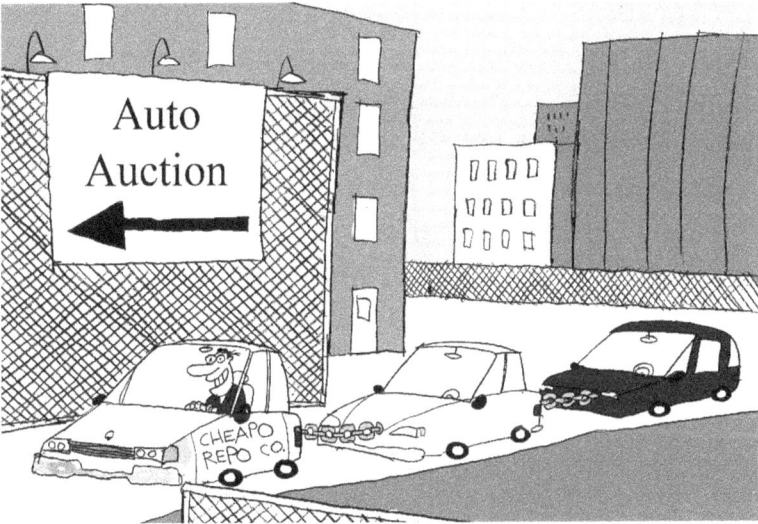

CHAPTER THREE

Vendor managers are always wondering how
Cheapo Repo Co. picks up invols
for $99 per unit.

Your First Repo Job

Getting a Job as a Repossession Agent

If you are new to the collateral industry, you need to look around in your area and find a repo company that is hiring. If you are having trouble finding a repossession company close to you, try searching this nationwide directory at *repoindustry. com/repo-directory.html* or Google auto repossession company plus the city and state in which you live.

Once you find some companies for whom you are interested in working, drop in and give them your resume. While you are there, ask to speak to the owner. Be honest and let him know if you do not have any experience in the repossession industry. But also, be sure to tell him that you are extremely teachable and eager to learn. If he tells you he is not hiring or does not want to hire you because of your lack of experience, try to offer to work for his company for very little or no money. Offer to ride along so you can be trained in the event that he does hire in the future. This will allow a chance for you to prove your worth to him.

If you do get the job, keep your mouth shut and your eyes and mind wide open. Do everything you are told and learn everything you can. Work for him for a long time and soak up all that you can in experience and knowledge. You may find that you can make a huge amount of money working for someone and never want to open your own repo business.

My Accidental Career in the Auto Repossession Industry

I can remember the night that launched my life into the wild world of the auto repossession business like it was yesterday. My first encounter with a repoman was on a cold day in the middle of winter. I met him at a local auto auction. He was there to drop off his latest "repo," and he struck up a long conversation with me. I was both irritated and bothered by him and his talking. The only thing I knew about "the repoman" was what I had seen watching the cult classic of the same name, starring Emilio Estevez. I never would have considered working as a repoman—not in a million years.

After the repoman dropped his repossessed vehicle into the storage lot, we went for a coffee and a chat. He ended up talking for a few hours, telling me some stories about the auto repossession business. I learned that I could make five times or more than what I was currently making in fewer hours. Shortly before he left, he handed me a business card and popped a question: "Would you like to repo cars in the area for me?" From that moment on, my world was about to be changed forever!

After a few phone calls negotiating what I was to be compensated for each car I repossessed, I met with the boss of my new repoman friend. He ran his auto repossession business from his house and had several storage lots located around the state. I remember thinking to myself that his repo company must have been doing fairly well, judging by the size of his house, his pool, his sports cars, and his extensive gun collection. I later found out that he owned several vacation and beach homes around the country. Not until several months later would I find out how he was able to enjoy such a wealthy lifestyle.

We sat in his home office, drinking coffee and talking about the auto repossession business. He was a thin man in his 70s, who claimed to have worked for the CIA, the Mossad, and other organizations that neither you nor I have ever heard of. The guy could weave a fairly good yarn, but I did not care, as I anticipated making a lot of money working for him. I did not believe a word of what he said and chalked his stories up to his being a talkative old man. As he shared his stories, he also included a crash course on "how to be a repoman." He then introduced me to his manager for further training.

My Quick and Easy Repossession Training Class

So I met with my repoman "trainer" for a crash course on how to repossess cars. Not only did he manage the company, but he also repossessed cars, served as a skip tracer, and even delivered cars to the auction. What he taught me was some old-school repoman training—no self-loader, no GPS, no laptop—only you, the debtor's car, and a tool bag full of goodies.

In those days, cars were not equipped with transponders or airbags, and usually they did not have an alarm to alert the debtor that you were repossessing his car. He patiently took the time to show me how to use a steering wheel puller, pound a socket onto an ignition and force it to start the vehicle, how to

YOUR FIRST REPO JOB

dent-pull an ignition and get it started with a screwdriver, and how to use those crazy old Ford passkeys. He had me go through the process several times to be sure I knew what I was doing, and then it was time to get my repo on! It really was not nearly enough training, but that was all I was going to get! I must say that I would not have been a success in this business without the instruction, advice and friendship that he gave me after that first quick course. If you want to make it in this business, find a man like this and learn everything you can.

When you go to work for a repossession company, you do need to make sure you do not get the short end of the stick like I did when it came to training! Ask all kinds of questions and make sure you thoroughly understand before you are cut loose into the field.

If you feel you need more training, don't be afraid to speak up. If you receive resistance, assure the person training you or the owner that you want to do the best job possible for them while taking safety precautions, and you feel that some more training will ensure that performance. The owner should really appreciate that sentiment and give you the best training you could possibly receive.

A FULL MOON FOR MY FIRST NIGHT OUT REPOSSESSING CARS

"Here you are," the owner of the auto repossession company said as he handed me a stack of repossession orders. I was thinking, *A little more training would have been nice, but he seems to think I'm ready.* As I looked through the repo orders,

I planned the night's strategy. I had teamed up with a friend to do the repossessions. We had agreed on a 60/40 split of the pay, since we were going to use my car. We loaded up our tools and headed out into the warm night. In the full moon, we spotted our first car right away. I grabbed my flashlight and bailed out to check my very first VIN. The VIN matched my repo paperwork, the keys were in the ignition, and the license plates were off the vehicle. The debtor seemingly knew the repoman was coming! The only problem was that both front tires were flat, so I called out the company wrecker to haul it back to the yard. So my first auto repossession was handled without a problem, and I was off to check some more addresses.

I worked two days repossessing cars with my partner, and we earned an even $900. After the split, I had made $540 and had only spent about $40 in gas. In only two days of work, I had made more than working all week at my regular job. My friend and I decided to concentrate on repossessing cars as many hours a day as we could.

I began to do the math in my head. If I could make an extra $1,000 a week repossessing cars, I could put my full-time job's check into a savings account and live off my repo income. Actually not just live, but live large! We decided to ask our new boss for some more work.

The boss was more than happy to pile on the auto repossession orders, and we were more than happy to add to our pile of cash! We were not lazy; we were honest, and most of all, we got the job done. He was happy, and my partner and I were both grinning from ear to ear! We were making so much money repossessing cars part-time that we had even thought of quitting our day jobs. Our full-time job was seemingly getting in the way of our getting rich from our part-time auto repossession gig. The repo orders kept coming, and the checks kept getting bigger and bigger!

My auto repossession partner and I were amassing a small fortune from all of our hard work. We loved the job, the boss was happy, and we were able to provide for our families like we had never thought we would be able to. The thought that we were going to be blessed with an endless supply of repossession orders seemed very possible.

I remember one particular night like it was yesterday. We had a huge stack of repossession orders come over the fax machine and were preparing to hit the street and pick up some cars. Have you ever asked yourself the question, "Is this too good to be true?"

DID YOU CHOOSE THE RIGHT COMPANY?

A few months into your new job, you might find yourself wondering if you made the right choice coming to work for this repossession company. Some of the factor to be considered include the following:

- Does the owner support you in your continued training and mentoring?
- Is his equipment safe and well-maintained?

And the big one—

- Are your checks cashing or bouncing?

The auto repossession industry is famous for not paying their agents on time. Sometimes the clients are slow to pay for their services, and the company experiences a cash-flow problem. Other times, the repo company owner handles his business budgeting poorly. He might simply be overextended on wrecker loans or other bills, or he may just be a jerk who pays himself before paying his employees! Make sure you find a repo company that pays you on time every pay day without a hiccup.

THE STEAK DINNER PAYOFF THAT WAS MEANT TO EASE OUR PAIN!

For several months we made a lot of money repossessing cars for our new boss. Our pickup rate was always over 90 percent, and our-less-than-perfect rate was not because we could not find the other 10 percent. The ones we did not repossess usually paid up, which resulted in our earning a close fee. Once in a great while we had an order that stumped us, but I do not believe anyone could have retrieved the car vehicle.

The memory of the day our boss rang me up and asked to meet with us in person seems like it was yesterday. We met in the parking lot of a truck stop. He slowly got out of his car and walked toward us with an envelope in his hand. He congratulated us on a job well done, handed me the envelope, and said, "I've included a little extra for you and your partner to go out and have a nice steak." After he left, I checked the envelope, and besides our check, he had included an extra $250. I guess he was expecting us to get a big steak!!

We went out for a nice dinner with our cash tip and had enough left over to fill up our gas tank several times. We were both thinking that we had a boss who appreciated our hard work and high recovery rate. He often commented that no other repoman who had ever worked for him had such a consistent high recovery rate like we had. As we rolled around checking addresses on our repossession orders, we talked about being able to retire early with a huge amount of cash in savings. We thought, *If we can repossess cars for just 15 years, we will be set!*

The savings accumulated from our auto repossession checks combined with some other business ventures in which we were involved would allow us to have a life of financial security by the time we were in our 40s. That night we repossessed and delivered six cars; we were on cloud nine! The next day we went to the bank and deposited our paychecks.

Both my partner and I received notices from our banks that our auto repossession paychecks had been returned for non-sufficient funds. We immediately rang the boss, and he explained away the problem. He said, "Sorry, guys. I forgot to transfer money from our operating account into our payroll account. I will transfer the money today and drop both checks in the mail this afternoon."

I pushed him to meet with us to get the checks hand delivered, and I offered to meet him anywhere. He whined that he could not meet us because he had a doctor's appointment. The guy was as old as dirt, so we decided to accept his promise to mail us the checks. Later that night we went out and repossessed four more cars.

The check was in the mail, but the cash was not in the account! We received and deposited our new rubber paychecks into our already lean bank accounts. We had no idea that we were about to receive some more NSF notifications sent to us, so we kept repossessing a boatload of cars for our "friend."

Apparently, our employer did not know how to manage his money. He lived in a beautiful home, had some nice cars and a slew of recreational toys. I am not sure what he was spending all his money on, but it was not on paying us! He did not have enough money to operate his auto repossession business while waiting for the banks to pay. The time had come to take some drastic action to get the money we had earned.

Our boss was into us for a couple of checks in the thousands of dollars and kept making excuses as to why we had not been paid. None of his excuses ever named him as being at fault. His justifications included a bank error with his business account, a mail error, and a lender's check that had bounced. He even had the audacity to blame us a few times. We were picking up too many cars, and he could not afford that kind of volume. Since he was not paying, we were not going to be going out and repossessing anything more until our pay was straightened out. We did, however, have a few "hostages" to bargain with—a motorcycle and two cars that he had said had to be delivered to auction right away.

He kept calling us and telling us to get all three to the auction, and that one debtor wanted to redeem his property. When we pushed back on NOT doing so until we were paid, he angrily agreed to meet us with cash. Even though he finally paid us, we refused to work anymore unless a better solution was set up. We negotiated getting prepaid for the cars we went to pick up. The owner was willing to prepay us to repossess fifteen units. With that guarantee, we went right back to work!

Are you wondering why we decided to work for this shady repossession company owner? I am not surprised that you are because we kept asking ourselves the same question. Of course, the answer came down to money—nothing more, nothing less. Despite being a conman, his auto repossession business had the lion's share of the repo work in our area, and we repossessed automobiles for all of the big lenders and the local banks. He knew how to talk to clients and keep them happy with excellent customer service. He was also an excellent skip tracer, and his company had a reputation for always getting the collateral repossessed. His downfall was that he managed money poorly and was not really good at paying his repo agents in a timely manner.

As far as our decision to keep repossessing cars? He paid well, and he also paid close and investigation fees. We were also repossessing cars the old-fashioned way—without a wrecker, and he willingly paid for any gas we put into the cars we repossessed, as long as we turned in receipts. We picked up fifteen units rather quickly, and he topped off his prepaid repossession agents for another round of fifteen repossessions. So far, so good! As far as our decision to keep repossessing cars under those conditions? I would not do it again today, but back then, I was young and did not know any better.

Eventually, I met an owner of another repossession company who was located a few hours away from where I was. They paid better and even had better accounts than the current company

I was working for. The other plus was that this company also provided its repossession agents with a wrecker! This plus was before self-loaders were hitting the market, so I was going to be given an older style L arm wrecker to use and receive $140 per car. I was given a second wrecker for my driver, and he earned $100 for each car he picked up. The owners were also willing to give me an additional $40 per car for managing the area and taking care of personal property and debtor redemptions. They even rented us a nice office and storage lot located about five minutes from my house!

Eventually, as with most things in life, things went south with that company. The owner ended up retiring and sold the company to his sons, who took possession and changed everything. Working for them no longer made good business sense. I hired on at another repossession company. Soon after, the owner approached me about buying his company. I did, and the company grew from two wreckers, a rollback, one office, two employees and sixty repos a month to three offices, a huge fleet of trucks, many employees, and hundreds of repos a month.

CHAPTER FOUR

Bubba calls it
"repossessing in stealth mode."

WHAT DO I NEED?

I WANT TO BEGIN this chapter assuming that you have already worked for someone else. You know how to the job, how the old repo company you used to work for ran the business, what you will incorporate from observing how they operated, and how you are planning to operate your company differently.

What do you need to get started in owning your very own auto-repossession business? No stealth mode equipment is available that will camouflage your wrecker from the public! So don't be Googling any towing disguises or anything like that.

I have often been asked that very question: what do I need to get into the auto-repossession business? The initial reply that often comes to my mind but has never left my lips is, "A lifelong membership to the Hair Club for Men, a good psychiatrist, a top-notch brawling divorce lawyer, the ability to sleep on the floorboard of a wrecker, and lastly, an abundance of patience and perseverance!"

Seriously, besides those tongue-in-check suggestions, you must have some basics to operate a successful repossession company. This chapter will address exactly what you will need. In subsequent chapters, I may touch on some of the items mentioned in the list and how to optimize them in the daily operations of your repossession business.

THE RIGHT KIND OF INSURANCE

Proper insurance for your repossession business includes the following limits and coverage:

■ **Commercial Auto Liability** (including Drive Away) $1,000,000–$3,000,000 to cover vehicle collisions in which you are liable. Drive Away is normally covered under the Non-Owned Auto Liability. Coverage for Physical Damage to your scheduled autos subject to the deductible of your choice can be included.

■ **General Liability** (including wrongful repo) $1,000,000 –$3,000,000. This insurance covers your assault and battery (unless excluded in your policy), your slipping and falling in the office, your car falling off the lift on to someone's foot claim. The split limits are per occurrence and annual aggregate, meaning you have $1,000,000 in coverage for any one claim up to three times per year.

■ **Garage Keepers Direct Primary** $375,000 (this limit is often dictated by the bank). Garage Keepers coverage has the most variety of claim types within the repossession insurance package. The most common claim and the greatest exposure for the company involve weather-related claims, i.e., a hailstorm damages every vehicle stored at your lot. This insurance will also cover the physical damage to collateral during a drive away claim or, of course, theft of collateral off of your lot.

The Direct Primary coverage now required by most lenders does not require your being legally liable for damage to collateral in order for your insurance company to pay a claim. This may at times make you angry and also put losses on your loss history that will affect your future premium.

- **On-Hook** $100,000–$300,000. In its simplest terms, On-Hook is exactly as it says—coverage provided to you to cover the collateral while a vehicle is physically attached to your tow truck. The devil is in the details on this coverage and can get you into trouble. Some say that it is simply the insurance company's made-up word to charge you more for your premium, and some carriers do not even offer this coverage. This coverage varies widely based on the form on which it is written. It may or may not cover "cargo," which means you have to read the specific carrier definition of what "cargo" is. The carriers that do not offer this coverage provide it under the **Garage Keepers** portion under the belief that the wording "care, custody, or control" extends this coverage to collateral on the back of your trucks because you cannot be in much more "care, custody, or control."

- **Employee Dishonesty Bond** (third party) $1,000,000. In theory, this coverage is to provide the lending institution with peace of mind in case your employees steal their collateral while it is in your possession. This bond was created in response to the gap in coverage created in the **Garage Keepers** form because it excludes coverage to theft by employees, owners, and officers. Problems with bonds that no one seems to tell you: there is at least a prosecution clause and most likely now there is a conviction clause in the bond. What this means to you is that in order for you to collect on your bond, the offender must be at least prosecuted and most likely convicted of the crime committed.

Bonds are not cheap and pay your insurance agent up to a 30-percent commission. Your standard commercial crime insurance policy covering employee dishonesty is half to a quarter of the price and only pays 10 percent. Some of the association bonds are not actually bonds but a financial guarantee of the association, stating that the member's net worth is X amount of millions and that, if needed, they can access that money through a special assessment of membership. Last but not least is that the bond still excludes coverage to owners and corporate officers. So if you are a small business, no coverage may be provided to you with this policy.

The insurance certificate must state vehicle repossession coverage on the policy, including wrongful repossession. You also need to have towing insurance if you plan on engaging in the business of doing private party towing, transporting vehicles to auctions, and other activities that might not be covered in many repossession insurance policies. Keep in mind that insurance limits and coverage are dictated by the lenders and clients. Some want more, and some want less.

In the current insurance marketplace, some companies do not want you running the same truck as a for-hire towing and repossession rig. Some are perfectly fine with covering multiple exposures at the same time, including even putting a snow plow on the front of your rig in the winter. This is when you need to partner with an insurance agent who will ask you the right questions to make sure that everything is disclosed up front to the carrier so there is no problem at claim time.

Under no circumstance would I suggest that you have multiple insurance policies covering the same vehicle—not two commercial policies, not a commercial and personal policy because you use your 3500 with a sneaker unit for personal use to take your family camping. Doing so can cause "stacking of limits" and an absolute nightmare during a claim. The limits that you carry need to come from two conversations that you have with your agent. The first and most important is to discuss what your exposure is and how to best cover it. For example, if you are small, you may only have three pieces of collateral on your lot versus a large company with 120 pieces. The next conversation is one of contracts. The business auto and general liability limits seem to be standard language through every lender. The **Garage Keepers, On Hook,** and **Bond** will all vary through the contracts. So you will end up with two limits—exposure limit and contract limit. You want to make sure you are carrying the greater of the two.

A COMMERCIAL OFFICE

The office you lease or buy needs to have secure doors and windows. A separate area will be needed for debtors to come to your business to claim the personal property that was in the collateral at the time the repossession was executed. Interior offices that are not accessible or seen by the public will be needed to protect the personal information of debtors from which you are repossessing collateral.

A commercial office will also protect you and your staff members from agitated debtors who might become violent. An important feature that your office should have is a locked room where you can organize and store property that is removed from the debtors' collateral. A definite plus is an office with some bays so you can do maintenance work and repairs on your wreckers.

Keep in mind that you may need to expand in the future, so select a location that can handle expansion. One final consideration is location. Find a centrally located office in your service area that is also close to the auctions where you will be delivering collateral. Being close to the auctions can save you thousands of dollars a year in fuel costs, wear and tear on your trucks, and paid man hours.

Tastefully decorate your office and keep it clean and organized. You will be there 50 to 60 hours a week, and your working environment can actually affect how you come across when you talk on the phone. If your office is disorganized, you and your staff will send out a disorganized vibe over the phone when dealing with your clients.

A Secure Storage Lot

Your storage lot will need to have at least a secure six-foot fence with three or four strands of barbed wire on top of it. It needs to have a gate through which you can get your trucks in and out that can be secured with a lock. Your lot should be paved or have asphalt or gravel as a ground surface. It needs to have electric service so you can install dusk-to-dawn lights, security cameras, and an alarm system. Any repossession storage lot can be broken into, but you want to fortify yours the best you can. Keep your storage lot locked at all times and never let debtors inside the fences. You never want to make it easy for a thief to get in by cutting corners.

A STATE LICENSE FOR OPERATION

If your state requires a license for operating a repossession company, you will need to obtain one. Visit your state's government website or call the state government office to find out what the current requirements are when it comes to licensing or other requirements. Consider taking their repossession company compliance program. The four states that are most recognized for having licensing requirements for repossession businesses, company owners, and repossession agents include California, Florida, Illinois and Louisiana. Things are always changing, so make sure you do your research.

A BUSINESS LICENSE

Obtain a business license if one is offered in the location where you are setting up your office. Some counties located in rural areas do not offer business licenses unless you are located in the city limits.

A PROFESSIONAL TELEPHONE, COMPUTER SYSTEM, AND COMMUNICATIONS NETWORK

Be sure to get an actual business line and not a residential one for your business phone line. You do not want to be calling clients and have them see "John Doe" on their caller ID; you want them to see XYZ Repossession Company. You will want to have business Internet to ensure adequate speeds to conduct business via your computers. You will need a fax machine/printer with capabilities for scanning and photocopying as well. You will also want to be able to communicate in the field with your agents, so require them to have or set them up with laptops and cellular phones. Your phone system, the first impression that new clients will have of your business, is an ongoing impression for your current clients. Remember, everything is either first-class or no-class.

Computers for Your Office and Laptops for Your Wreckers and Camera Cars

Purchase decent ones that have reviews stating they can take a beating and keep on ticking. Make sure they have a top-of-the-line antivirus installed, they are password protected, and they are professionally mounted.

A Recognized and Widely Accepted Repossession Management Software System

This system will be utilized to receive and send repossession orders, communicate with clients, submit condition reports, bill clients, etc. Every client seemingly has one he likes, and often, a repossession company will have to utilize multiple repossession software systems in order to get assignments. I know of a couple of repossession companies that only accept faxed orders. This policy surprises me, but these are small one-man operations with only a few clients. However, these companies seriously limit their growth by only accepting faxes.

The following is a current list of repossession software systems being used in the industry:

- National Agency Management Systems LLC NAMS
- Recovery Database Network, Inc RDN
- IRepo

- Prios
- Recovery Manager Pro
- Repo Systems
- Re-Pros
- VA Repo
- RepoXR
- Baja Recovery Software
- My Recovery Systems

A Professionally Designed and Easily Navigated Website

In this day and age, any business owner would be foolish not to have a website. You can't have a billboard erected in front of hundreds of lenders' offices, but with the right type of search engine optimization and Internet marketing campaign, you can reach thousands of lenders 24 hours a day. The site should have an online complaint form for debtors to file a complaint if they would like to do so. Several email addresses should be set up with your website domain name. You should not be using Gmail, Yahoo or AOL as your business email. Doing so appears unprofessional and indicates a mixing of your personal and business life.

RepoStudMuffin@nonbizemail.com is not going to score you any points either! Set up some email addresses such as sales@, updates@, and one for the owner. Be sure that whoever sets up your website forwards all company emails to your private email account. People, especially those in the repossession industry, get busy and forget to check their company email, so receiving alerts to your phone so you don't miss anything important is wise for the business.

DECENT-LOOKING AND WELL-RUNNING EQUIPMENT

Your equipment does not have to be brand-new, but you should always keep the equipment that you own detailed and looking nice. Your local clients will see your trucks around town, and you want your trucks to have an appearance that instills confidence in your business.

You will need at least one wrecker and one rollback to be able to effectively run your repossession business. The wrecker should be a self-loader for picking up vehicles from debtors and bringing them back to your secure storage lot. Wrecker styles vary from manufacturer to manufacturer, and everyone, including me, has his favorite.

Although I prefer a wrecker body, other types of trucks that have a sneaker lift mounted below the rear bumper can be obtained. Make sure you check your state's requirements on trucks that can be used for towing. I always like a dually truck, but some of these sneaker units are mounted on trucks with just two tires on the rear axle. The rollback can be used for hauling all-wheel drive vehicles, transporting two pieces of collateral at a time to the auction, and picking up voluntary surrenders. All of your wreckers should be equipped with wheel dollies and the highest quality straps, ratchets, and chains you can find.

AN LPR (LICENSE PLATE RECOGNITION) CAMERA SYSTEM

The system should be mounted on an energy-efficient car to scan license plates in your coverage area. Many clients actually require that their adjusters have an LPR system. You can also use your camera car as a spotter vehicle to save the money it costs to run a "gas-hog" wrecker. Multiple LPR systems are available on the market. I will not recommend any by name, but I will advise you to do some extensive research before you choose one. LPR cameras are a huge investment, and you do not want to make a mistake when choosing which system you will be using.

You will want to check into how many clients the LPR company has loading active repos into their system, how good (or bad) the company handles customer service, the pay rate for a repo, the length of time to pay, and if you get paid per plate scanned or for historical data. Be sure to find out if the LPR license plate data collected is owned by you, the LPR company or both, if the LPR company requires your signing an exclusive deal with them or whether or not they will allow you to run more than one LPR system without any problems, if the company works for the good of the industry or for themselves, and the cost, if possible, of financing the purchase of LPR cameras. List the pros and cons for all the LPR companies and choose the one that is the best match for you and your repossession company.

CLEARPLAN

Clearplan is a real time logistics tool that maps, tracks involuntary, voluntary and other repossession related tasks with icons that monitor and display account activity by your agents. It also communicates with many of the repossession management software systems so you can update accounts seamlessly through the Clearplan system.

MAGNETIC TRACKERS/GPS UNITS

Find a reliable magnetic trackers/GPS Unit that does not have monthly fees but has a very long battery life. Your camera car drivers or agents can place them on a vehicle that is up for repossession that they can't get to or might drive away before they can secure it. Then the collateral can be tracked to its new location and picked up there.

KEY-CUTTING MACHINES AND KEY PROGRAMMERS

Key-cutting and programming machines are available for lease or purchase. Personally, I would purchase new machines rather than used ones. Having a key machine and learning to cut and program keys can allow you to offer that service rather than contract out to a locksmith.

A TOP-NOTCH, PROFESSIONAL OFFICE STAFF

The office staff must be willing to answer the phone quickly and handle their business. The staff you have in your office will be the "face" of your company that the clients see every time they call your office or get a call from your office. Find people who project a positive, organized, caring and hardworking image when they communicate via phone. Remember the old adage that you get what you pay for, and be sure you pay enough to get the type of person described in this paragraph.

CASH RESERVES

You will need plenty of cash reserves to keep your auto repossession company afloat. When you repossess a piece of collateral, the repossession fee that you charge is not paid the same day, same week, and sometimes not the same month! I had some clients who paid me the day after the repossession was executed, but that practice was not the norm. In fact, some clients pay 30 to 60 and sometimes even 90 days after they are invoiced. Some have to be re-invoiced and repeatedly called again and again for months to get them to pay. While you are waiting for your money to be paid, you will have to pay the bills to keep the business operating. You will need a substantial amount of cash flow to pay your office and storage lot rent, truck payments, fuel costs, employee salaries, and other business costs that won't be able to wait for you to get paid.

Oftentimes, repossession company owners have secured or unsecured lines of credit to meet short-term working capital needs. If you make the decision to attain these types of loans, keep the following thoughts in mind. You will be charged interest on the money that you borrow, and this fee will eat into your profits. So try to pay the amount borrowed before the interest kicks in. This might be tough, but if you stay organized and make sure you pay on time, it can be done.

You need to pay these loans down each time a client pays you so you can use the money you are allowed to borrow when operating funds run low. Be sure you use the money only when you have to and never use it for anything other than the operating expenses of your business.

Don't spend the money on personal items! I know a few business owners who have used this loan money to go on cruises, to buy Harley Davidson motorcycles and even diamonds and jewelry for their wives or girlfriends. They failed to remember that this money represents cash flow to cover the daily operations of their business until they obtain the receivables that are due to them.

CHAPTER FIVE

"I only charge $150 an ivol,
so I can't afford to use my wrecker!"

What Do I Charge for My Repossession Services?

I KNEW A repossession company owner who always had at least one of his wreckers on jacks in his shop. Seriously, every time I visited him, I would walk in his shop and see at least one of his trucks on jack stands or with the hood up and parts all over the place. One time I visited him twice in one month, and the same truck was sitting there all torn apart both times I was there.

"Hey, are you waiting on parts?" I asked.

"No! I am waiting on checks from several clients so I can get it repaired and back on the road."

I joked, "Maybe you should get rid of your wreckers and simply drive all of the cars you repossess back to the shop."

He chuckled. "Right…but what if the car doesn't run. How am I going to get it back to my storage yard?"

I laughed and suggested, "Push it all the way; it will be good exercise!"

"Well, maybe I need to go play the lottery so I can afford to get this old truck fixed."

I happen to know that he did like to gamble a bit too much. Wisdom is remembering that business is not a gamble or buying a lottery ticket.

When you are in business, you have to make money—a lot of money. If you don't charge enough for your repossession services, you won't last very long in the business.

Every new repo business owner is looking to get as much business as possible when he first opens up. Bringing a lot of business in the door certainly must mean that you making a lot of money, right? Not always! You need to be sure that you are charging appropriate fees for your services. *An appropriate fee* is code for "a fee that always makes you profitable." Remember, there is a difference between making a profit and making a living. If you are an employee, you can be somewhat satisfied in making a living, but when you are a business owner, you need to make a profit—and hopefully, a huge profit!

If you invest in the stock market, you would not be happy if you only earned a 1 percent or a 2 percent return on your investment, would you? You definitely would not want to lose money in the stock market, right? You would want to make a huge return on the stocks in which you have invested! If you bought a house for $150,000, you would not want to keep and properly maintain it for 15 or 20 years and sell it for $100,000. No! You would want to double or triple your money!

I have invested in a few stocks over the years, and I have found stocks are not my strong suit. In fact, I lost money every time! I would read books on the stock market, research individual stocks, talk to stock investor gurus, and religiously follow my broker's advice. None of my doing due diligence ever helped me.

On the advice of my broker, I invested in a medical stock

that was close to receiving FDA approval on a life-saving device. The stock was trading at somewhere around a nickel a share but had days where it would go up to 15 or 20 cents a share. I bought some shares and began to watch the market closely. At one point, it climbed to over 50 cents a share. I excitedly called my broker to sell, but he talked me out of it because he had heard it was weeks away from getting FDA approval His thought was that it could go to $15 a share or even more. I did some figuring and told him to hold. Six weeks later, the announcement came out that the company did not get FDA approval. Soon after that the company bankrupted and closed its doors. Those losses hurt enough that I did not keep ringing my stock broker to give him *free* money.

Besides being a repossession company owner, I was and am also a real estate investor. I also studied and learned the business of the real estate market very well and was very profitable in that arena. I could quickly crunch the numbers and know right away what kind of profit or loss I could make on flipping a house. When someone told me what he would sell me a house that I was considering keeping as a rental, I could immediately know what the monthly cash flow would be. Like my auto repossession business, I was extremely successful at flipping houses and buying properties for rentals.

Being a repo business owner is not any different than investing in stocks or being a real estate investor. You will invest a substantial amount of money in your new venture, and as with any investment, you will need to make a return on that investment. You need to look at your business just like any other investment, whether it is stocks, mutual funds, real estate, or whatever else a person may have in his portfolio.

You also have to realize that although it may seem like your business is making a lot of money, you need to factor in for future emergencies and expansion, as well as business maintenance costs.

A future emergency may be as insignificant as a flat tire on your wrecker or as costly as the motor locking up on the same truck. If you are renting an office and a storage yard, your landlord may decide not to renew your lease when it expires. That would mean you may have to relocate and move your entire office and operation to another location. That unexpected expense could become quite costly.

Every business wants to expand and grow, and you need to be making enough profit to cover future expansion. What if you land a major account that sends you so much work that you need to purchase two more wreckers to run those accounts properly? Were your past profits enough to make those purchases? Profits should cover future expansion for the down payments for needed trucks, or even better, enough cash to pay for two used or new wreckers. You may need to rent a remote office or one or more remote storage lots. Rents, down payments, and additional insurance costs are never inexpensive.

Business maintenance includes upkeep on office equipment, towing equipment and the business office. All of these areas need to look first-class and operate professionally. Maintenance costs money that most new business owners never even consider.

To the majority of people, $100,000 to $150,000 represents a considerable sum of money. Yes, that would be a decent amount to pay yourself as the president and owner of your auto repossession business. You could also pay your wife another $40,000 a year for running your office. You may think that those combined salaries are great, and they are great wages for living; however, they are not profitable!

When you own a business, you should be able to pay yourself a decent living wage, but the business should also make a decent profit. If you need to buy three new wreckers, that $150,000 a year is gone right away. If you blow a motor or two and have some other equipment repairs, that may add up to another $6,000 to $12,000. At that point, you and your wife are earning around $28,000 to $34,000 a year to operate a business. At the low end, that is close to making less than the wages the two of you would make if you were working for a fast-food restaurant or in a retail store. Hopefully, you can see the difference between making a *profit* and making a *living*. When you look at those numbers, you should be able to see that your business will have to make a profit on top of paying yourself a salary.

Of course, when you first go into business, you probably will not be able to pay yourself a six-figure income along with your company making a huge profit, but you will need to set your service fees high enough so those kinds of numbers can be realized in the future. Look to the future and decide where you want to be financially personally and in the business. Set some goals, crunch the numbers, and make a plan.

So what should you charge for your professional repossession services in order to be profitable? First, let me share some percentages that will lead you on your way to profitability.

A recommended business profitability percentage equation target could be 33.3 percent funneled into three categories that I call *the percentages of the thirds*:

1] 33.3%.......... Business operations
2] 33.3%.......... Salaries
3] 33.3%.......... Business profit

Of course, in the beginning, when first starting your business, you may need to adjust the formula to a 50% / 25% /25% split. You may even have to make more of an adjustment to the percentages, but you should never have a business profitability percentage that is much less than 25 percent. And that number should grow in time until you meet the percentages of thirds. Reaching those percentages may take years, but you must plan ahead and work toward those numbers to be successful.

You are probably still wondering the specifics as to what dollar amounts you should be charging for your clients to repossess a car. This fee would vary from state to state and even from city to city. It can be greatly affected when comparing urban areas to rural areas.

The first advice I can give you is to never, ever give away free services. When you figure what you are going to charge for an involuntary repossession, you should figure in the following services:

- The repossession itself
- Storage

- Key-cutting charges
- Completing a condition report
- Bagging and tagging the debtor's personal property
- The storage of the collateral
- Transportation of the collateral to the auction
- Meeting debtors who are picking up property or redeeming their vehicle if they have paid it current

When coming up with your fee schedule, you also need to figure in gas prices, employee costs, insurance costs, your office and storage lot costs, your utility costs, your equipment costs, and other incidental fees.

Some years ago I kept hearing talk of involuntary repossession fees of $275 to $300 and sometimes even lower. Using *the-percentages-of-thirds* formula for a $300 fee, then $100 would be designated for each category. Does the math add up to profitability when you look at a $300 involuntary repossession fee? Can you run your repossession business at that rate, grow the business, and pay yourself well enough to cover your personal bills?

I can attest to this much: in 1990, auto repossession companies were getting $350 for an involuntary repossession, plus a key-cutting fee and a transport-to-auction fee. Daily fees for storing the collateral at your lot and oftentimes even mileage fees and investigative fees were also accrued. Back then, lenders sometimes paid a full involuntary repossession fee if the repossession agent got the debtor to bring his loan current and most paid something decent for that. Many clients paid a close fee if the agent worked an account and the debtor or the collateral could not be found. Those were the days!

In the mid-1990s, I saw some fees closer to $400, and some as high as $425 for an involuntary repossession. The total inflation rate from 1994 to 2014 was 61.36605 percent. At that inflation rate, you would think that the cost of an involuntary auto repossession should be more like $550 rather than $275 or $300. How did the repossession industry see such a shocking decrease in fees? The price of gas in 1990 was around $1.16 a gallon. I know wreckers and rollbacks were significantly cheaper, and I'm sure that insurance and the cost of an office and storage lot were also significantly less expensive.

So with all of these figures in place, what should you charge per auto repossession? Do the math and figure out what you need in order to make it in business. Each person's circumstance is different than the next person. Some prospective business people may already own an office building and storage lot free and clear. Others may already own some towing equipment. Other people reading this book may be debt-free personally and not need as much to be profitable. Some people like a higher society style of living, while others may live a simpler life. When I owned my auto repossession company, I had very few bills, owned several rental properties, and my lifestyle was simple and relatively inexpensive. I did not need the $60,000 sports car, a Hummer, and a mansion to feel important and cool. In fact, I have always driven a used vehicle and have been content with every house I have lived in.

In the end, the prices you charge will also have to be competitive with the market price in your area. Whatever you do, do not go around undercutting your competitors to get business, which is one of the main reasons for the profitability death that the repo industry has experienced. Those undercutting company owners come in, force the price to be lowered, steal some business, and then go out of business because they had no idea what the cost of doing business was.

I know some repossession company owners that have showed me some of their invoices and have seen some involuntary prices at $375. Then they tack on bag and tag fees, key-cutting costs, and a delivery-to-auction fee bringing the total fee for a repo closer to $500. Some also charge daily storage fees. If you can get close to that $450 or $500 mark for an involuntary repossession, then you are reaching the profitability mark that you need to hit to be a business owner who makes a profit rather one who is simply making a living. For voluntary repossessions, I would suggest half of that fee.

Of course, the above-suggested fees are my opinion only and based on what I think needs to be charged to be profitable. I do not know what repo agencies in your area are charging. It could be more than that, or it could be a whole lot less. You will need to do some research to find out what the going market fee for your area is before you come up with a fee structure for your company.

CONTINGENCY WORK

Many clients want their collateral picked up on a contingency basis, which means that you will only get paid if you repossess the collateral. This model of payment can be costly as you may put a lot of legwork into finding a car and never locate it. Try to get a client to pay you some sort of a close fee, if he is willing to do so.

SKIP ACCOUNTS

Sometimes you will get an account that has been out for re-possession for months and months. Maybe one, two or ten other repossession companies had the account and were unable to find it. Charge a lot more for these skip accounts. If several other repo companies worked and could not find it, you will have to allocate numerous hours into locating this repo.

SKIP TRACING

If you plan to do any kind of in-depth skip tracing on an account, then you need to let the client know you plan to bill them for that work. Do not do any skip tracing for free. If the client refuses to pay for it, then refuse to do it. They will need to provide you with accurate address information if they want the collateral recovered.

OVERSIZED AND SPECIALTY COLLATERAL

When a lender asks for a quote on an RV, a camper, a boat, a yacht, a semi-tractor, any heavy equipment such as a bulldozer or a crane, or any other specialty piece of collateral, be sure to figure in every factor before responding. You may need a trailer to pick up a boat or construction equipment. Will you rent it, or have you already shelled out some big money for it? Does your agent require a CDL to drive a semi, or will you need a wrecker big enough to tow it back? How many agents will you send? Is it a camper that is hooked up or secured on a pad at a camp site? How much time and work will it take to get the camper ready for transport? Are all of the RV or camper tires aired up and road worthy, or are you going to have to go buy tires, take the old one off and mount new ones? How many spots will the collateral take up in the storage yard?

Remember, you can always go work for a repossession company and make a very good living. The repossession agents I employed who were really good at what they were doing earned close to that six-figure mark every year. They made great money without all of the business owner-associated headaches or stress. If you are the repo-company owner, you will have an abundance of them, so consider investing in some Extra-strength Tylenol and Yoga classes! If you are planning to put yourself through all of that, then you better make sure that you are very well compensated—more than just making a living!

An employee only puts in his time; a business owner puts in his time, plus his money, blood, sweat and tears. He commits his life, his financial wellbeing, and so much more. The business owner puts his rear end on the line with all the financial risks that come with owning a business. He always faces the chance of going bankrupt, lawsuits, losing his family, not to mention the toll on his physical and mental health. The employee shows up, works some hours, and goes home. He gets his check every week and worries about what is on HBO on Friday night or who will go all the way to the World Series. I am saying to make sure you are making enough of a profit to make the risk worth it all.

CHAPTER SIX

"Green 1974 Pontiac Grand Ville...
RO is Jimmy Hoffa...
this must be an order from a forwarder."

TYPES OF CLIENTS

EVERY NEW BUSINESS owner is looking to get as much business as possible when they first open up. However, let me advise you that you should be selective in the types of clients for whom you want to work. You should never do work for a lender that you lose money on. Never work for a client that is going to hurt your company financially. As I have already mentioned in the previous chapter, you need to make a profit with this business—not just a living.

So now that you have your auto repossession company packet, you are going to need to know what types of clients are available for you to target. The following is a brief list of clients to whom you should consider trying to sell your services:

- **Nationwide Auto Finance Companies** like Ford Motor Credit and others that write auto loans in all fifty states or a large number of states. These clients can be extremely profitable for your business because of the sheer number of repossession accounts they may have in your area. Keep in mind that many nationwide lenders do not pay any type of close fee if you are unsuccessful in picking up the collateral.

- **Nationwide Banks** such as Chase Bank and others that

write auto loans in all 50 states or a large number of states. These clients can also be extremely profitable for your business when it comes to getting lots of work. Just like nationwide lenders, many nationwide banks do not pay any type of close fee if you are unsuccessful in picking up the collateral.

- **Local Banks** in your hometown or state. These can be the most profitable for the fee that you can charge for an involuntary auto repossession. They are often more willing to pay close/cure fees. I know several that still pay investigative and mileage fees as well. One great benefit to having a local bank as a client is that they are close, and you can develop a strong personal relationship with the collections manager and his staff. They often pay their bills quickly, which is good for the cash flow of your business.

- **Local Credit Unions** in your hometown or state. Just like your local banks, a local credit union can also be quite profitable for involuntary auto repossession fees. They are also often more willing to pay fees other lenders seem not to want to pay in the current repossession industry climate. Strong personal relationships with the collections manager and credit union staff can also be formed. They are also generally very quick to pay bills.

- **Local Finance Companies** in your hometown or state. They are comparable to your local banks and credit unions when it comes to fees and relationships that can be made. They may also ask you to detail and sell cars for them. That would be your decision, and if you do so, be sure you know and abide by your local and state laws when it comes to selling collateral.

- **Title Loan Companies.** They may have a lot of work and may pay well. Some of their collateral may be tougher to locate than some of the previous clients listed. Some repossession company owners hate them and won't do their work, and others claim they have become rich off of doing their work.

- **Local "Buy-Here, Pay-Here" Car Lots.** They often pay quickly in cash, but finding their collateral can sometimes be difficult. Some company owners hate them and refuse to do their work. I know others who love them and claim they pay better than more conventional banks and auto finance companies.

- **Auto Repossession Forwarding Companies.** Forwarding companies seem to be the most controversial companies to do repossession work for. Essentially, they are the middle man for some lenders and repossession companies. They often pay less than what repossession company owners want to be paid. Although everyone constantly complains about them, I rarely meet a repossession company owner who refuses to do their work. One plus is that they often have a substantial amount of work for their adjusters. Also a large majority of lenders no longer perform direct repossession work, which means they will not deal directly with a repossession company. They will not choose a repo company to use, issue them repossession assignments, or communicate with them at all. They let the forwarder handle everything and communicate only with them.

ARE YOU WORTHY ENOUGH TO BE THEIR REPOSSESSION CONTRACTOR?

Lenders are selective on who they use to perform their repossessions and do their due diligence before they start doing business with a company. Make sure that you have the "right stuff" to be worthy of their hire. You better have enough equipment, as well as decent equipment and all the necessary tools, to get the job done the way they expect it to be done. You must have the correct criteria to meet their requirements, such as a physical office, a secure storage lot, the required insurance and bonding, compliance training and continuing education for you and your employees, and other qualifications they want. You will need to have a decent reputation for being great repossessors, for honesty and integrity, for professionalism, for a good safety record, for a good turnaround time, and for your stellar customer service.

IS THE CLIENT WORTHY OF YOUR SERVICES?

The clients expect a great deal from their repossession contractors, but on the same token, what do you expect from a client? You should also have some standards and requirements for who those with whom you choose to do business in the repossession industry. It always made me wonder why repossession company owners do not check out lenders before they agree to do work for them.

Some criteria for deciding if you want to do work for a particular lender include the following:

- Do they pay their adjusters fairly?

- Do they pay their contractors close or cure fees?

- Do they pay their repossession companies in a timely manner, or will you be waiting to get paid three months down the road?

- Do they compensate the repossession companies that they use for their services, or do they expect a long list of freebies?

- How long have they been in business?

- How much "paper" do they write, and how many repossession orders do they issue on average in your area?

- Do they have a stellar reputation?

- Are they loyal to their repossession contractors?

- Is the repossession fee price point their number-one concern, or are they willing to pay a fair fee for professionalism?

- How do they treat their contractors? Like a partner or like their pawn?

You can sometimes learn these answers by asking the collections manager. Even if you get some answers that you are looking for, you should also go on the Internet to see if there are any complaints or compliments about the client. Check out some repossession industry-related websites like *repoindustry.com* to see what repo company owners and agents are saying about a client. At *repoindusry.com* you can view and also ask questions in a private forum that we have set up to discuss lenders. Since this forum is private, the repossession company owners and their employees can feel free to discuss clients without worrying that what they talk about will be seen by those clients. Two categories, "Client Score Cards" and "Client Reviews," which will help you with your decision about a client are located on the forum at *www.repoindustry.com.*

If you do not see a particular client you are investigating, you can post a new topic so agents can see it and respond with their experiences with this lender.

You should also talk to other repo company owners from associations to which you belong or ones with whom you have developed a professional relationship over the years. Of course, it may not be best to ask your competitor up the road. He does not want to lose a client to you, so he will likely not tell you the truth!

CHAPTER SEVEN

Visiting a Client

O NE OF THE things that is missing in the auto repossession world is building personal relationships. I am not talking about "business buying" and bribery, which is what I have sometimes heard when this subject arises. I am not sure why some people would even think that, but it certainly reveals that they do not know a lot about business.

People simply like to do business with people they know and trust. You would not choose some guy off the Internet to build a deck for you if some guy you have known for twenty year who attends your church owns the "Friendly Deck Building Business." In all likelihood, you would use your friend from church. You see him often, and you trust him. After all, he has built decks for half of the people in your congregation, and everybody loves his work! You would not think to use someone with whom you did not have such a great relationship.

Why is the repossession industry different? It should not be, but for some odd reason it is. I have heard of clients becoming suspicious or even rude when asked to meet for lunch. How can a client and a repossession company owner do business together if the only interaction they ever have is an email? How trust is ever built with a faceless entity is beyond my comprehension. How can solid trust be built if the only time a client calls a repo company owner is when he received a phone call from some debtor he has never met complaining about a scratch on the vehicle that was repossessed.

As a repossession owner, you need to work on building long-lasting, strong relationships with your clients. As a lender collections manager, you should want to do the very same thing. Nothing is wrong with developing relationships; in fact, it makes for better service that can last a lifetime.

Meeting with a Client

A personal visit to a client is an excellent way to build a working relationship. The visit could entail making an appointment to stop by the office or maybe grabbing a lunch together. Of course, if you are in New York and the client's office is in Texas, a personal visit may be tough to put together. However, even if the client is far away, I recommend trying to make a yearly visit if possible. If the client is local, more frequent meetings can be more appropriate and are needed.

Getting together in person not only builds relationships, but provides an opportunity to do a quality check on the services you are providing. When you meet, find out what is or is not working for the client. Encourage the person to be transparent and assure him that you can and will fix any issue. Make no unattainable or empty promises to them. If the issue is something you cannot do, be honest and let the client know and explain why. Remember what you promised and make sure you when you get back to your office, to follow through in implementing what you said you would do.

———

DRESSING FOR SUCCESS

I have seen some real fashion disasters worn by auto repossession company owners going to meet with a lender. I was visiting one of my clients when one of my competitors dropped in unannounced to try to get some repossession orders. He showed up in jeans with holes in the knees, a "wife-beater" t-shirt, a wallet chain, and a pair of flip flops. He wore a dirty ball cap with "Porn Star" printed on it. I am not sure if he had bathed or brushed his teeth that morning, but he smelled like recycled summer sausage!

I have been told I am a great storyteller when telling about this business owner. How I wish I were simply sharing a story, but it did happen. Needless to say, he never got one order from my client and was soon up for repossession himself.

Cold sales calls, emails, and letters are great, but to be successful in any business, you need to build personal relationships. A personal relationship in business, where faces are connected, handshakes are exchanged, and bread is broken, makes for lasting business clients. In order to begin this relationship building, a face-to-face meet and greet needs to be made if at all possible. Oftentimes, the size of the auto finance companies makes this impossible, but if at all possible, make it happen.

When you make a personal visit to a potential or current client, remember that your appearance does matter. When presenting your company, you should always dress appropriately. Leave the Metallica shirt at home. You are the owner of a company and not a "repo man" when you are making a sales call.

I have had many people tell me that all they wear are Harley Davidson shirts, jeans and boots, and they are not changing who they are for anybody. Great. I often wore "biker attire" myself. However, in all my years in business, I have made a discovery: people react to what you are wearing. If you show up anywhere in a ketchup-stained tank top and shorts, you will be treated much differently than the man who is wearing pressed Dockers trousers, a buttoned-down shirt, and some business casual shoes.

I came to this revelation some years back in my daily trips to my bank to take care of personal and business transactions. I found that if I went into the bank looking like I just fell off the mattress, I was treated exactly how I looked. I was barely greeted, there was no smile, no chitchat, and even the customer service was substandard. However, when I entered the bank in casual business attire or, once in a while, wearing a nice suit jacket and tie, they fell all over me. They greeted me, they smiled, they were in a hurry to assist me, and sometimes they told me I was looking fine!

Some of you may assert, "Well, they should treat all customers the same!"

I agree 100 percent; however, the reality is that it does not happen that way. Shortly after I made my discovery that your appearance will determine how you are treated, that particular bank approached me and offered me an unsecured business line of $60,000 to use for payroll if some of my clients were slow to pay. Was it because of how I dressed when I went in there? I am not 100 percent sure, but I would say my appearance definitely played a big part in it.

I am not saying you need to wear a suit all the time, but I am saying to dress for the occasion. If you are going jogging, wear a jogging suit, t-shirt, and tennis shoes. If you are going on a poker run on your "hog," put on your leather chaps and a Harley shirt—but do not forget to wear a pair of jeans under those leather chaps! And if you are going to meet with a lender, dress appropriately if you want your auto repossession business to grow.

So I ask again, "What is appropriate dress for meeting with a lender?" Is it a suit or sports coat and dress slacks? I would say no. You are a repossession agent, and honestly, I can't ever remember meeting a client who was wearing a suit. You do not want to dress better than the client you are meeting, so I am suggesting you wear casual business attire, like a pair of dress slacks or khaki Dockers with a pressed, buttoned-down shirt. You will also want to be sure you have showered, slapped on a little antiperspirant, combed your hair, brushed your teeth, and ironed your clothes.

The following scenarios are examples of what to wear and what not to wear when you are trying to get clients to use your auto repossession business or visiting clients who already use your repossession service.

GRABBING LUNCH WITH A CLIENT

Meeting for lunch with a potential or current client is an excellent way to grow your auto repossession business. Eating with a client sets the scene for a casual and intimate connection. This setting can bring about a bonding experience leading toward a long-lasting business relationship. Of course, you need to handle yourself professionally and socially for this to happen. Eating with someone will bring familiarity to the relationship, exposing your manners (good or bad), weaknesses and strengths. Your conduct will either strengthen the relationship or ruin it. Before making an invitation for lunch, you need to determine if your client can fit the meeting into his schedule. Some collection managers are so frequently bombarded with lunch offers that they make it a practice not to accept any invitations. If they can't meet you somewhere for lunch or don't have the time, then offer to meet them at their office.

When you invite a client to lunch, you need to make the purpose of the meeting very clear. Do not act as if you just want to hang out and shoot the bull. Make it clear that you are paying for the meal by saying, "I'd like to take you to lunch" or "Please allow XYZ Recovery to buy you lunch." Do not flippantly say, "Let's do lunch" as it will leave him wondering who is going to pick up the tab. A good invitation would be: "I'd like to meet with you and talk about (insert your purpose). May I come and see you sometime? Or could you break away from your busy day to let me take you to lunch?"

Be sure you choose a place to eat that is appropriate for a business lunch! You will want to avoid noisy places, restaurants located in areas plagued by traffic congestion, and certainly, seedy strip clubs or hole-in-the-wall bars! Find a restaurant with an inviting atmosphere. The location should be close to your client's office and convenient for him. The meeting place should be chosen with only him in mind and not you. As the host, you should be the one to choose the venue, unless he outright requests a certain restaurant.

The following is a list of considerations when making your restaurant choice:

- Remember if it is not first-class, it's no-class!

- Choose one that serves a variety of cuisines such as a café, bistro, or steak house.

- Be sure your client will be able to choose a dish he likes.

- Choose one that you have been to before and know that the food is tasty and the customer service is first-class.

- Choose a place that is clean, has a relaxed atmosphere, and, most importantly, is quiet.

- If the meeting is out of your area, search the Internet for restaurants with great reviews.

- Know in advance how the restaurant accepts payment—cash, check or charge.

Be sure to make a reservation so you are not waiting in the restaurant lobby for 20 or 30 minutes because no tables are available! Nothing is worse than looking like a poor planner by ending up having to go somewhere else to eat because your client can't spare the time for the 50-minute queue for a table. Also be sure to reserve a quiet table for your meeting. Arrive at the restaurant at least ten minutes before the scheduled time. Use the restroom when you arrive so you do not have to excuse yourself during the lunch. You should allow the hostess to seat you and tell her to be on the lookout for your client. While you are waiting, have a word with your waitress. Inform her that this is a business lunch and you would like her to bring you the bill. Also request that she keep interruptions to a minimum, but not to sacrifice customer service in doing so. Promise her a healthy tip for her service. Once you have your table secured, you may go to the restaurant lobby and wait for your guest to arrive. When he arrives, allow him to follow the hostess to the table and let him choose his seat.

LUNCH RULES

- Shut off your mobile phone.
- Give your undivided attention to your guest and the meeting.
- If he makes the first move and orders alcohol, then you may, as well, but go light on the booze with just one.
- If he is pounding the drinks, you should still sip yours and not even get remotely close to being intoxicated.
- If he orders a drink and you are not a drinker, just tell the waitress that you will have water for now.
- Don't smoke.
- Match your client's meal. If he has a three-course meal, then you should do the same.
- Try to order something similar so your plates will arrive at the same time.
- When you choose your food, be sure you order food that is not messy but easy to eat. I would recommend

not ordering anything like Saganaki flaming cheese, barbecued ribs, or Oysters Rockefeller!

GETTING DOWN TO BUSINESS

Do not attack him with business talk as he is sitting down. You need to wait for an appropriate time to talk shop. For new clients, spend some time getting to know each other. For a current client, take some time to catch up since your last meeting. Enjoy some light conversation minus any talk about politics or other touchy subjects. Sports, travel, and hobbies are excellent subjects for conversation. Continue to hold off on talking business until your meals have been ordered.

A great time to talk business is between the salad or appetizer and the main course. When the bill comes, casually pick it up, place your credit card in the bill holder, and close it. This should be done with absolutely no effort or attention drawn to it. The day after your lunch meeting, you should send the client a short note, thanking him for taking the time out of his busy schedule to meet with you.

Writing a handwritten note or card is a forgotten art, and I suggest resurrecting the art and giving it a try. Receiving a personal and unforgettable handwritten note certainly has to be a better experience for the client than getting some quick email. A handwritten note will have a major impact and can have a powerful message.

CHAPTER EIGHT

Marketing Your Company

YOU HAVE ALREADY invested a substantial amount of money into an office, office equipment, auto repossession insurance, wreckers, and other needed tools to operate a successful auto repossession business. Marketing your auto repossession business does not have to be as expensive as you might think. When it comes to marketing, the repossession industry is a whole different animal from any other business out there.

You need clients, and you want to get your repo company noticed, but unlike other businesses, you won't be advertising on billboards, the radio, or on television. Of course you won't want to do anything silly like a K-Mart blue-light special, offering the first 5 repos at 20 percent off or other similar embarrassing promotions!

You might then be wondering, "How can I advertise my repo business effectively?"

When I was in the auto-repossession business, I wanted my clients to be thinking about me all of the time. I wanted to brand myself to them in every way possible. I often said that if I could, I would have urinal and stall advertisements in their company bathrooms; plates, bowls, coffee cups, and napkins in every single client's break room; and a billboard in front of every collection manager's house so when they left for work and returned home, they would be thinking about my company!

Many ways exist to promote your repossession business besides making sales calls and sending out packets to potential clients. Most people in the repossession industry cannot afford to hire a marketing firm or a dedicated salesman to work for them. That said, you need to have a marketing plan that is always working for you. An inexpensive tool that will work for you 24 hours a day and 365 days a year without needing a vacation or day off is a website. You won't have to pay it a commission, and it won't be asking for overtime or a health-care plan. A website is one of the best tools with the most economical investment that you can get for your business.

You would certainly be smiling from ear to ear if you made an additional $7,000 every month off of an investment that cost you a minimal fee. Investors in the stock market would love to invest just $500 to $1,000 and get $7,000 every month as a return on that initial $500 investment.

If you do not have a professional website built, then you are missing the train on something that will bring you an abundance of business. Who in their right mind would not make a small investment that results in big money coming their way? Often repossession company owners offer a great deal of opposition when they hear of the need for a website. Oftentimes, when they see that they need a website, they somehow find "Cheapo Website" to build them ugliest website known to man for a minimal fee. My friend, when you are in business, you need to come to terms with the fact that you will need to spend a little on advertising in order to build your business.

Let me be frank. Many of you reading this book right now are spending a whole lot more on coffee over a year's time than you would spend on a professional website. Many of you freely spend money on cable television, satellite radio, cigarettes, chew, coffee, fast food, and all manner of things that are not building your business in any way, shape, or form. These things that you easily spend money on are not giving you any return on investment, yet you do not hold your wallet close to your chest when it comes to these expenditures.

I am not against spending money on entertainment, but I am against doing so when you do not even think about having some sort of advertising budget for your company. I hate to hear a guy express to me that he cannot afford something that costs very little that would bring him more business. We all can afford to find the cash to bring more revenue into our businesses. We all spend money on the "feel goods" of life, and here is a news flash—an extra $7,000 a month is a big "feel good" for any business owner!

I have talked with hundreds of extremely successful auto repossession company owners who have told me the same figures over and over. They have shared that their website reels in as many as twenty or more orders every single month from lenders who find their website online. Many times, the order is a one-hit wonder, and they never do another repossession from that lender ever again; however, many of them have brought on a high-volume lender who found them through their Internet presence. All of the repossession company owners who have business success stories always have a first-class website.

They advertise on all of the auto repossession company directories, have good content, and, in time, rise to the top of page one of Google. These owners have wreckers, offices, storage lots, repossession insurance, and all the "must haves," but they also have an online presence. They have an advertising budget, market their companies, make sales calls, and spend money to build something great. These guys are the "riches" part of the "rags-to-riches" stories about which I hear.

While I was writing this chapter, I spoke to a repossession company owner based in Tennessee. He has followed this Internet marketing advice for the last couple of years. He actually told me that he is turning down clients and can be selective in deciding for whom to do work. He claimed that a great majority of his client base came as a result of his website and the Internet marketing he did for his repossession business.

On the other end of the "rags-to-riches" stories are those who will always have the "rags." These are the countless repossession business owners with whom I have talked who are "dying on the vine" and crying the blues about not making a profit. These owners have wreckers, offices, storage lots, repossession insurance, and all the "must haves," but they do not have a website or an online presence. They do not have an advertising budget, they don't market their companies, they do not make sales calls, and they resolutely refuse to spend some money to build something great.

What is the one big difference between the people with

whom I talk? One group is like a cigar boat flying over the waves of a smooth, blue ocean. The other is like a boat that is taking on water, listing to one side, and slowly but surely, sinking. The good news for the second group is that I am sharing with you what I hear on a daily basis about what is building repossession businesses. I am telling you what I know that actually works.

If you are not yet convinced, the following is a list of additional reasons why you need to build a first-class, professional auto repossession company website:

■ **A website will always improve your company image.** Clients are bound to ask you for your website address, and if you do not have one, then you need to have some solid reasons to tell them why you don't. Telling them it is too expensive certainly will not help your image! Every one of your current and potential clients will have a website. Why don't you have one?

■ **A website can help get your company some exposure.** Having a website is essentially like having a billboard on every street, in every city, town, and neighborhood, and in every state of the country. A website gets you noticed, which results in more business.

■ **A website can reduce costs because it is a permanent, non-print brochure for clients to view.** There are no mailings, design or printing costs when a client visits your repossession company website to view your "online brochure."

▨ **A website is always working**—24 hours a day, 7 days a week, 365 days a year.

▨ **A website offers your clients and potential clients choices.** They can call you at the contact number listed on your site. They can find and utilize your fax number on your site, or they can send an email. A potential client can find you through Google or other search engines and have several ways to contact you when they need an auto repossession done in your service area.

▨ **A website makes you competitive.** If a potential client is looking online for a repossession agent in your area and you do not have a website for them to find, then I give you a 150 percent chance of *not* getting that repossession assignment! If you have a company website and no one else in your area has one, then you are bound to get work from clients searching your area for an agent. If you have a site and some of your local competitors also have sites, then at least you have a chance to compete for business.

▨ **A website is like a window that clients can look through to take a peek into your business.** Most nationwide clients are probably not going to stop by your office to say, "Hello," but they can stop by online to visit you. If you include some professional photos of your operations and offer some rich textual information about your repossession business, then they are able to get to see "the real you" and how you operate your business.

A website, like anything else, takes time to work. Relevant and fresh content, blog posting, search engine optimization, good key words, link exchanges, pay-per-click ads, and length of time online will help to move you up the Google search ladder. You do not want to start a website and shut down one month later simply because you did not get 100 new repossession orders off of your new site. You need to be patient to see the fruit that results from having an online presence.

To make a good company website, be sure your content clearly states your mission and the site is easy to navigate. The clients should know exactly what your auto repossession company can do for them. The website also needs to get your logo out there and project an online image of what your real-world business is all about.

A potential client who lands on your website needs to know what you can do for him. Make the content short and concise. No one wants to wade through a novel of text to find out what services you provide. A viewer should not have to work to find what he is looking for.

Have a classic-looking website. Do not be too flashy with blinking lights or loud music blaring at your viewers. Very few people like to suddenly have music blasting at them while they are working at their desk. They also do not want to look at a site that is visually loud in color and design. Your site should look like a professional business site—not a blog, banner farm or Facebook page.

Your site should be inviting to your viewers. When they arrive, they should feel like they are in the lobby of your office or a five-star hotel that is welcoming them to come inside and stay for a while. They should feel at home when they visit your website.

Your company website should be free of grammatical and spelling errors. Before publishing your site, you need to proofread your site multiple times and also have someone else proofread it. A second set of proofing eyes will always find errors that the first proofreader misses. Oftentimes, the original author misses his own errors when he proofreads what he wrote. I have found this to be true when I write an article.

Your site should make contacting you very easy. Place your email address, physical address, mailing address, and company phone number all throughout your site. You also should have a "Contact-Us" link and page on your site that will take the viewer to all of your contact information.

Last but not least, maintain your website by keeping it free of spam, broken links, errors and other pesky problems that annoy viewers and cause you to appear unprofessional.

AUTO REPOSSESSION COMPANY DIRECTORY

Another way to promote your business online is to list your company on every website that has a state-by-state auto repossession business directory. Several directories are online, and your business needs to be listed on all of them. These ads can link back to your website and help raise it in the search engine rankings, which will bring more clients to your website who are looking for companies in your coverage area. Lenders who use these directories will also be able to find your company when they search one of these directories for a repossession business in your area.

If they are looking on one of the directories for a repossession company in Chicago, Illinois, for instance, they can see your listing and choose to use you. If they are doing a simple Google search for a repossession company in Chicago, Illinois, then they may get search results for your repossession company from your website or three or four different repossession companies from the state-by-state directory.

Again, I cannot stress enough to list your company on every repossession company directory on the Internet. If a top spot in a state is available, grab it and never let it go. That would mean you will always be seen at the top of the state in which you will be listing your company. Being at the top of the state is definitely worth whatever is being charged for the ad, so don't be shy about spending the money.

Here is a link to sign up your company in our directory: *repoindustry.com/pre-registration.php.* At the time of the printing of this book, you can list your company for as little as 17¢ a day ($79.95 for 15 months) for a basic listing and roughly 32¢ a day ($149.95 for 15 months) for a top state listing. Obviously that fee is much cheaper than that cup of coffee you buy at Starbucks every day, and you will actually make money off of the pennies you invest each day.

Free 5-Year Company Listing Available

If you bought this book, I will give you a free 5-year listing for your company. To take advantage of this offer, forward your book receipt to *repoindustry@gmail.com* and add the text "free5 in the email subject bar." Then, go sign the register for your free listing with the email address you used to forward your book receipt at *repoindustry.com/pre-registration.php*. When it asks you to pay, DO NOT pay, and within 24 hours, my staff will manually approve your listing for 5 years.

OTHER WAYS TO MARKET YOUR COMPANY

The following ideas are several additional ways to market your company. Some of the items on the list are free, some are inexpensive, and some are costly. All of them have a huge potential to bring clients to your business.

▪ **Set up a free Internet business listing** with *Google.com/local/, Bing.com/local/,* and *listings.local.yahoo.com/*. Include a link to your website and a description of your company.

▪ **Set up a business profile page** on Linkedin, Facebook and Twitter, and be active on those sites.

▪ **Seek the assistance of a printer to design some professional business cards, a company packet, letterhead and envelopes.** Always carry business cards with you. You never know whom you are going to meet. I know of one repossession company owner who went to a fund raiser and met a man who was in upper management of a nationwide finance company. He never, in a million moons, expected to meet a prospective client at this meeting. If he had not carried business cards, he might have had to write his contact information on a dirty napkin and probably would not be picking up an average of 75 cars a month over the last 5 years from that finance company.

■ **Have a PowerPoint digital packet created to send via email.** It will be a lot cheaper if you can do it yourself, but do not attempt to do so unless you know how to create one and can make it look first-class.

■ **Have a professional one-minute DVD made about your company** with video of your office, equipment, storage lot, and staff. Include a brief message from the owner, talking about the benefits of using your repossession company. This DVD can be included in the company packets you send out, can be uploaded on YouTube, and can be sent via email. If you have a professional camcorder or camera with video capabilities, video editing software, and the knowledge on how to create videos, it will save you a lot of money. However, just like the PowerPoint presentation, do not attempt to do so unless you know how and can make it look first-class.

■ **Make sales calls as often as you can.** Do not be afraid of the dreaded "cold call" because they can't kill you; they can only say yes or no.

■ **Join professional business associations,** such as the Chamber of Commerce, Rotary Club, or other civic associations. You are bound to make some contacts there, as well as get personal satisfaction from being a member of these worthwhile organizations.

■ **Join a professional auto repossession association** or join an auto repossession compliance company.

■ **Send out online press releases about your company.**

▦ **Attend auto repossession, skip tracing, and other industry-related seminars.** If you are a Subject Matter Expert (SME) on some an industry-related subject, you can also offer to speak at some of these seminars, branding yourself as a professional in the repossession world.

▦ **Write an article for an online repossession industry-related, towing, or auto lending website or hard copy publication.**

▦ **Network with other repossession agents online and in person.** This industry could be great if we all learned to lend a helping hand to each other.

At all times, act accordingly and professionally in your business and personal life. You and your equipment can be your best and worst commercial! I know of one repossession company owner who recently got into a road-rage situation while driving his wrecker. He was quite depressed to realize he had flipped off one of the top members of the board of directors of a credit union for whom he did work. As a result, he lost that lucrative account, which averaged 25 repossessions a month—that is pickups, not repossession orders! Not including transport and key fees, he lost over $10,000 a month in revenue. Now that is one expensive finger gesture!

BRANDING YOUR COMPANY

The key to getting business is to always be branding your business. Besides making phone calls, you should routinely drop a business card and a brochure in the mail to potential clients to keep the name of your company in the back of their mind. You will want them to think of you first when they are ready to change repossession companies.

I was always big on branding by using small promotional gifts to win clients. You can effectively promote your company by sending the collections manager and his office staff some gifts with your company name on them. Imagine that the collections manager receives a bad report about his current contractor. Now upset, he heads into his office for a cup of coffee and grabs your branded company coffee mug that you sent two months ago. He then sits down at his computer and begins to use his mouse on a mouse pad you sent him a year ago that has your company name, phone number and logo on it. Then he picks up one of your company pens that you sent him last week. The next thing he will likely do is pick up the phone to call you to discuss bringing you on as a contractor! It is because he can't help but have your company name on his mind. It is seen all around him.

Giving away polo shirts, baseball caps and t-shirts displaying your company name and logo are a surefire way of increasing business. Most office dress is casual these days, and collectors appreciate receiving a nice polo shirt as a gift. If you give every customer service representative a polo shirt or a ball cap, then I can promise you that on any given day, you will be the most advertised repossession company in the office.

The best way to get business is to have your company name out there. In the repossession industry, it would be ineffective to rent a billboard to advertise your business. You have to create your own "billboards" on collectors' desks via coffee mugs, pens, clothes, and other office-related materials. You can argue that all of that advertising can be expensive. It can, but I can promise you that it pays for itself.

Some repossession company owners only give gifts when they already have the client. I think this is a good practice, but even better is giving a gift for no reason at all. That gift is the one that will make the collections manager think of your company. If you get your name out there and make a follow-up call every month, then I can almost guarantee that you will be repossessing for that lender in the future.

Employees at financial institutions come and go. I was able to land some big money contracts because someone left one lender to work for another company and took one of my coffee mugs with him when he cleaned out his desk. Later he was having coffee with his new boss, and they ended up having a discussion about my company. Within the week, I was signed on and doing so many repossessions for the new company that I had to go out and buy a new wrecker and hire another agent. This may not happen overnight, but I promise you that it will happen over time.

Keep in mind that giving out promotional gifts to potential clients could be an issue with that company's policies. Some companies do not allow their employees to receive any gifts from potential contractors or service providers they currently use to do their work. Some only allow a promotional gift if everyone in the office receives the same item. Others have a cost limit on the gifts they are given. You do not want to buy their business with gifts; you want to promote your business's name.

I went to Michigan to visit a lender's call center that had a lot of repossession work in my service area. I had a local "mom-and-pop" deliver enough pizza and soda to feed their entire collections staff and repossession department workers on their lunch break. I gave each collector one of my company mugs filled with personalized candy with my company logo on it. I walked around and visited each rep and asked them for input on what they wanted in the way of service from the repossession companies they used. I had a pad of paper and pen and jotted down what each one of them said. I listened intently, took in every word, and developed a bit of a rapport with each person I talked to that day. Later that evening, I had dinner with the executives of the call center to get their input as well. Nearly every person I talked to that day told me they never had a repossession company owner take the time to hear their needs and wants in service. They said many were rude to them and often seemed like they did not care about them at all.

I flew back that night, wondering if my sales visit had made an impact. The next morning, I arrived at my office to find my staff standing around the fax machine. Orders were literally spitting out all over the place! That day we received over 150 brand-new orders. For the rest of the time I owned my repossession company, I continued to receive a huge number of repossession orders from that client. I also gained four new major clients when staff from the first company left and went to work for other auto lenders across the nation.

CHAPTER NINE

The owner of Cheapo Repo Co.
has his hands in a lot of businesses.
He has to make money somehow....

EFFECTIVELY
MANAGING YOUR OFFICE

I F YOU WANT to operate a successful office, I cannot empha-size enough the importance of having updated equipment and technology. I understand that you may be attached to that 1950s manual typewriter and those ledger books, but it is time to move on! Your office should have up-to-date computers, software, fax machines, and phone systems. Always have plenty of toner for your fax machine and printers. Consider the wisdom of purchasing a back-up printer. You will be embarrassed if a lender is trying to fax you orders and you have to tell him that you are out of toner or your fax machine is broken.

Nothing irritates a client more than to be talking with someone in a repossession office and hearing them shuffling through hundreds of papers to find an update or a condition report. If someone on your staff will be talking to lenders, then that person needs to have a computer and an efficient database of all of the accounts that your company is running. However, it does no one any good to have an awesome database of information that has not been updated. You need to have an employee entering new updates and condition reports every morning so your staff is able to access that information from the database when the client calls.

Another facet of the business that lenders will not tolerate is always hearing voicemails. Install a phone system that will accommodate multiple lines and also roll over to available lines when others are busy. I use *grasshopper.com* for every company I own. I am about to create a third account for a new venture that's about to launch. Grasshopper is a virtual phone system that allows you to obtain a phone number for your business and forward it to wherever you want, including your home phone, your office phone, or even your cell phone. You begin by choosing a phone number to represent your business. This could be a local number to indicate you are part of your local community or a toll-free number to show a more "national" presence. To give your company more of an identity, you can search for a vanity toll-free number like 800-YOURBIZ. From there you can create a main greeting, which can sound very professional, that callers hear when they call your company. You can create and customize extensions to make your company seem a little bigger (think "press 1 for sales" and "2 for support") but still answer the calls in whatever location is convenient for you.

And Grasshopper is not solely for inbound calls. If you want to call a client, Grasshopper has an excellent mobile app that allows you to make calls using your Grasshopper phone number as the caller ID rather than your cell phone number. Your clients will never know you're calling them from your mobile phone. You can even send text messages from the app so that you can communicate with your customers on the channel that feels right for them.

If you choose Grasshopper, you won't have to change the phone system you are currently using. The program will work with any mobile, home and office phone set up you already have in place, so you won't have to buy phones or other equipment. Grasshopper is completely virtual and will transcribe and deliver all of your voicemails and faxes right to your email. You won't have to listen to a voicemail; you can instantly read the transcribed voicemail.

Grasshopper really provides quite a few primary values. The first is that it's an easy way to keep your work and personal lives separate and appear more professional. The second is that it allows you to work wherever and whenever business calls. Lastly, with the Grasshopper mobile app, you can respond to your customers more efficiently and deliver great customer service. All of these perks are invaluable to a small business and will help you grow and manage your business effectively.

Grasshopper has yet to fail me, and I have received calls via their system at home, driving, in my office, poolside, and in some of the most remote countries around the world. There are a lot of pieces to the puzzle that make a business owner and a business successful, and Grasshopper is one of those pieces.

You need to have enough staff to keep up with the call volume that you have as well. You can gauge how many employees you need in your office by the average number of calls each day. If you are receiving thirty voicemails every hour, then it is time to add staff members. If you are going to interact with clients on your cell phone, make sure you are in a quiet place where it can be done in a first-class manner. Nothing says that you are unprofessional more than when you are on the phone with a lender in your truck, and the employee working the drive-thru asks if you want to upsize your order!

Lastly, you need to have set office hours. You can't simply "shut the office down" because business happens to be slow. You never can tell when your office will get busy. Or worse than that, the largest lender in the country calls your office to offer you a lucrative contract, and their answer is a voicemail saying you closed early. You also may want to consider your hours based on the location of the lenders who use you. If you have major clients on the East Coast and the West Coast, then you might want to open earlier and close later in order to accommodate them.

I know implementing all of these suggestions can be expensive, and we hate to spend money if we do not have to. All I can say is that if you spend your money wisely, it can and will make you money. You do not have to go out and buy ten computers and hire eight more people for your office. Hire more people and buy more office equipment only as needed.

SCHEDULING AND STAFFING

Employee staff strength should be at a level to run operations smoothly and efficiently. Of course, you may get slammed on occasion, but for the most part, you will want to make sure your office is adequately staffed. You do not want calls going to voicemail; clients, transporters, debtors, and others subjected to being on hold for extended lengths of time; or important tasks not being completed because your staffing numbers are below par.

Of course, you should also ensure that your current staff is doing their part to get the job done before you hire additional people. Human nature is to take the path of least resistance and do less; therefore, you will need to make sure you keep your staff motivated to give it their all so you are not overstaffed with too many people doing too little work.

I remember one occasion when my office staff told me we needed to hire additional staff. This request came in about the same time as when one of the employees was about to get married. Seemingly every time I walked in the office, she was on the phone talking wedding plans with a florist, a cake bakery, her seamstress, her mom, or her fiancé. I cautioned her multiple times that taking care of personal business during office hours was unacceptable, only to walk in and find her making decorations for the wedding at her desk.

I am not one to stand in the way of love, but this employee's lack of regard for her work had become a huge burden on the company and the other employees. As much as I believe in the development of employees through "train, retrain, train again, and train once more before handing someone a pink slip, I did end up letting this staff member go shortly before her wedding. She simply would not get in line with the role and job she had been assigned. In all truthfulness, her wedding planning had become far more important to her than doing the job I was paying her to do. Needless to say, my wife received an invitation to the wedding, but I did not!

DOWNTIME FOR THE WORKERS

Dealing with debtors, clients and other calls in conjunction with being in front of a computer all day can be both physically and mentally taxing. Staring at a computer screen for extended periods can lead to eye strain, neck pain, and headaches. Sitting too long in an office chair can cause lower back issues, poor circulation, and numbness. Your staff will perform at their optimum level when they are given adequate breaks and a lunch. If the space is available, have a small break room with a kitchen and some vending machines. Eating lunch or taking a break at one's desk is fruitless and not a real break. You might even consider having a picnic table in your storage lot so your staff can go outside for some fresh air on days when the weather permits.

These small considerations are important to the morale of your team, and the law guarantees a certain amount of time for both. Make sure that they are implemented. Also make sure that these privileges are not abused.

You may not need to do this yet, but as you grow, I would recommend your operating your office staff on two shifts. I would start the first shift in the early morning, perhaps starting at 5:00 a.m. and ending at 1:00 p.m. The second shift, of course, would be from 1:00 p.m. to 9:00 p.m. The early shift will have time from 5:00 a.m. to 8:00 or 9:00 a.m. to prepare information for the business day. Clients won't be awake during those early hours, and a plethora of work can be completed without the phone ringing off the hook and other interruptions interfering with what needs to be done. The second shift will also have a quieter time from maybe 5:00 or 6:00 p.m. until 9:00 p.m. to accomplish an abundance of work. This later time can be utilized to get all of the following day's repossession assignments issued to the agents. If someone were not working later hours, these assignments being made to the appropriate repo agents would have to be done the next day.

OPERATE A PROFESSIONAL, CUSTOMER-SERVICE-ORIENTED REPOSSESSION OFFICE

No matter what happens in the field with your agents, your office will always be on the front line with the lenders. Your agents will rarely interact with your clients, unless a debtor calls the lender and puts the agent on the phone with the collector. The professionalism of your company will be revealed each day from the time the bell rings until quitting time. Your office staff will set the tone of your whole company. If the office workers are sloppy and unprofessional, I can promise you will lose business.

Clients contacting your office need to know that they are calling a professional company—not just the "repo man." Even if your company is a small family-run business, the lender should never have that impression. Callers should not be able to tell the difference between calling your office or the office of a Fortune 500 company. Therefore, you need to hire and train professional office staff who are capable of interacting with lenders who will be contacting your business. They need to possess the appropriate interpersonal communication skills to relate information about accounts accurately and efficiently. Your staff needs to practice phone etiquette, patience, and computer skills, as well as have an ability to keep track of the multiple accounts that your company is working.

Lenders calling do not want to be on hold for hours, confused by inaccurate updates, or lied to. Dishonesty is the one element that will do irreparable damage to your company. I know that lenders can be overly persistent about their accounts, but that is their job. Your job is to secure their collateral or at least have good information as to why it has not been picked up yet. If your office staff is on the ball and professional, then you have already won most of the battle.

Make sure your staff are trained to be well-organized, customer-service-minded and professional. You may think your staff excels in doing their job, but you need to take a very close look to be sure that is actually the case. I spend all week returning calls to auto repossession company owners who have called my office seeking advice or looking for help in building their business. I am not calling them to sell something; I am calling them because they asked me to call them.

One element that seems to be a common denominator is that the people who answer the phone seem to have an attitude from the time they answer until the time the call ends. And let me be perfectly clear, I am so happy when those calls finally come to an end! Sometimes, I have the feeling that they are bothered that they even had to answer the phone to begin with. I can almost picture them scanning through Facebook, liking posts and commenting away, when suddenly the office phone rings and interrupts their work-time entertainment. How dare someone call the business when they are busy playing Candy

Crush Saga! Who would think that these angry employees who are paid to do a job would act so put off to actually earn their money by taking a call. This behavior does not take place once in a while; I encounter this attitude with close to 80 percent of all the calls I make to repossession companies.

THE GATEKEEPER MISTAKE

Another common denominator that I encounter when calling a repo company is being interrogated hatefully by the receptionist answering the phone when I ask to speak to the owner or manager whose call I am returning. Even if I know the person's name and explain that I am returning his call, I am treated hatefully. I am told by lenders that office staff often play "secret squirrel" with them as well. They ask for the owner, and the interrogation begins. If a lender asks for the owner or asks about his name, the staffer usually acts rude and refuses to give a name. I have been told this happens even after informing the employee that they are clients.

What employee in his right mind would act that way to a potential paying customer? What business owner would want his employees treating their clients that way?

KEEP AN EYE OUT

The owner needs to monitor his office staff's behavior when they are dealing with people on the phone. He might er-roneously be thinking that his employee is dealing with a rude or grumpy debtor, when the opposite is true. The truth is, the office staff should treat everyone who is calling with dignity and respect—even the poor debtor who had his only means of getting to and from work repossessed by the collection representative to the collections manager of your biggest client. The office staff never knows who will be calling.

AGENT/OFFICE STAFF RELATIONS

On a side note, the office staff needs to treat every agent, transporter and lot worker with respect too. I have seen mistreatment and have been a victim as well. Coworkers treating each other badly never builds a successful team. Bad behavior and bad relationships will negatively affect business.

I have seen office staff treat the field agents horribly. They act bothered to take a call from them or to discuss a particular account. I have heard them sigh, complain and roll their eyes when an agent calls in. I once saw a girl working in a repo company office put an agent on hold so she could "check" an account for him—only to purposely make him wait for what seemed like an eternity. She even thought sitting and doing nothing while this poor agent was held hostage on the other end of the phone line was extremely funny. She never checked any records, but finally picked up the line and told him there was no new information or updates. She even felt comfortable enough to treat that agent with that great disdain right in front of me—an outsider to the company,

I know that sometimes repo agents can be gruff and unfriendly, but I want to address office staff in this section. I will address agents in another chapter. Usually the office staff is the only point of contact the agent has with the client. They may need information, want to provide some additional info, request some skip work to be done on an account or other business-related material. The office staff needs to be trained on how to help the agents to the best of their ability. Not only that, they need to be pleasant while doing so. The auto repossession industry is already full of negativity and unpleasantness, so make sure the office staff is not adding to the misery.

CUSTOMER SERVICE TRAINING

Customer service training for employees is a necessity that is seriously lacking in nearly every repossession company. Owners need to consider enrolling their office staff in training that will beef up their customer service skills. He should also commit to doing in-house, hands-on customer service training with them. Doing monthly and quarterly evaluations on their performance, career development reviews and Performance Improvement Plans (PIP's) will encourage them to improve on identified deficiencies.

You might be thinking that all of these suggestions sound like a lot of work. They surely are! Being a business owner is a lot of work. Every owner should be a bulldog when it comes to protecting the business that provides for him and his family.

You might have the thought that you are only a small company and only large corporations take online and inhouse training and implement career development initiatives with employees. You are either a professional business owner or you are not! You need to run your operation like you would run a Fortune 500 Company as its CEO.

THE ATMOSPHERE

The atmosphere in your office can make or break your company. I am not talking about allowing employees to personalize their desks and have real plants! All that is a something you should allow. What I am talking about it about is the spirit in the office—the *vibe* if you will.

I once visited a repo company's office for only a few minutes and felt a deep sense of negativity. The company owner had called to ask for my help with his failing business and low morale issues among the employees. Later I found out that the owner was famous for screaming and cussing fits. He and his wife were having marital problems and fought all the time, and that antagonism was spreading like a cancer throughout the company. The company had called to ask for my help.

I suggested several changes, which were never implemented. Less than a year later, the owners divorced, both the husband and the wife filed bankruptcy, the doors closed on the business, and their beautiful home went into foreclosure. Both were brought up for repossession themselves.

LOSE THE "CORPORATE STINK"

I have been in some repossession companies where the owner treated his employees like expendable chattel. I remember one owner who had assigned negative names to his agents like "retard" and "dumb piece of (expletive redacted)." He was always saying this "one" or that "one" had one foot out the door. He threatened them, screamed at them, and belittled them. He did not care about them one bit. The employee turnover rate at his company was so high he could hardly keep track of who worked for him at the moment. His employees hated him, and all knew he equally hated them; I felt bad for all of them.

I always tried to treat my employees like family. I invested in them, loved them, and tried my best never to fire any of them. I am not sure if I took that desire too far or if I was ever taken advantage of, but we all sure enjoyed coming to work every day. I bought lunch for the office staff a couple of times a week, hosted company parties a few times a year, and made employee birthdays a big deal. I enjoyed the benefits of a great team.

Promote Teamwork

"Coming together is a beginning; keeping together is progress; working together is success." - Henry Ford

Why is teamwork important to your repossession business? A team works better than any one person can. Individuals who see themselves as an integral part of a team feel appreciated. Being appreciated brings them great happiness and self-confidence. Your company experiences greater productivity, loyalty and commitment. Teamwork causes employees to be more interactive, efficient and innovative in the workplace.

Having a great office team can be the difference between a mediocre repo company and a stellar repo company. If you can build a team of employees that enjoys coming to work, then you will be well on your way to having a successful business.

What are some steps company owners and managers can take to build a team?

- **Be a good leader.** Be the kind of boss for whom you would be thrilled to work.

- **Be a good example.** All eyes are on you, and how you act will influence the actions of your staff.

- **Be good communicators.** A confusing message is a recipe for disaster. Make sure all management agrees and conveys all communications and directives.

- **Be positive and upbeat.** Being positive and optimistic will rub off. Who wants to work in a negative office?

- **Clearly define each staff member's roles and duties.** Nothing is wrong with cross training employees, but having individual roles and duties makes employees "own" what they have to do.

- **Be encouraging.** Give lots of kudos and compliments when employees are performing to or above your expectations.

- **Be forgiving.** People make mistakes, but be sure to use positive correction to change behavior. Beating someone mercilessly with words will not fix anything.

- **Resolve conflict among staff immediately.** I once heard a repo company owner say he was not paid to babysit and did not want to hear about problems between staff. His was definitely the wrong choice!

- **Be open to suggestions and ideas from your staff members.** In fact, encourage them to be creative in the idea department.

- **Address unacceptable and uncooperative behavior right away.** Be calm, explain why they need to change their behavior, and remind them that they are an important part of the team.

- **Host a weekly office party.** The planning could entail something as simple as ordering in pizzas or one where all of the coworkers bring in a dish and beverages for a potluck meal.

- **Consider instituting compensation, bonuses, and reward programs for your employees.** I believe you will reap unexpected rewards when you institute any type of incentive program. Workers will perform more efficiently and do their work better and faster, and as a result, the customers will be increasingly satisfied.

Besides making a lot of money and having a successful business, one of the my most rewarding (and tearful) moments was the outpouring I received when I announced I had sold my repo company. I heard comments like, "I love working for you," "I have never enjoyed coming to work so much," and "This place has been like family. Now that you are leaving, it will never be the same." A few big and burly tough repossessors cried when they heard the news. For years, many of them have reached out to me with similar love and appreciation for how I operated the business. I know I was not always perfect and did a lot of things wrong, but my heart was there for not only the business, but for the family of staff who worked with me.

WHAT IS THE DEFINITION OF A TEAM?

Teams are described as "groups of people with complementary skill sets who work on projects or activities towards common goals." Team members are cooperative and interdependent.

How hard would it be to build a team for your business? Many people do not like the idea of being on teams. This dread of teamwork often stems from past experiences. Everyone has been on a team with that one person who did not contribute. Additionally, some managers force teams on people, without taking the necessary steps to ensure that the team members will work well together and develop chemistry, believing that they will magically work better. Teams that are not launched correctly have little chance of being successful. It is important to get teams off to a positive start from the very beginning by developing relationships, inspiring goals, and defining roles.

CHAPTER TEN

Clients—Cheapo Repo uses the highest quality
equipment to make sure it's your collateral
being picked up and not the wrong car...NOT!

Managing
Your Repossession Agents

MAKE SURE THAT your repossession agents working the field have the tools they need to get the job done safely and correctly.

I have seen auto repossession agents be unprepared to carry out the jobs assigned to them. I once watched one of my repo agents jump out of his truck to check the Vehicle Identification Number (VIN) on a car he was trying to repossess. His problem was that he had forgotten to bring his flashlight. He embarrassed himself in front of his boss by trying to read the VIN with a Bic lighter on a windy day. His lighter kept blowing out. He also forgot the VIN he was supposed to be checking! I watched him run back to his wrecker and fumble around looking for his repossession order in the most disorganized mess of paperwork I have ever seen.

To top the evening off, I noticed he was wearing a pair of flip flops performing a task that was nowhere near the beach. He could have had a chain or other heavy item fall on his feet. The debtor could have run out, jumped in the vehicle, and run over his feet when he drove off. This agent's career in the repossession industry did not last long.

On the flipside, I have also had the pleasure of observing my prized agent, Ron, pulling cars like an artist. Every time I watched Ron repossess a vehicle, he always had all the tools he needed on each and every repossession. I watched him use a floor jack to work an Explorer out of a tight spot. I witnessed his using a variety of mechanic's tools to get the job done many times. On many occasions, I observed his spraying down his flatbed deck with a water and soap solution so the vehicle would easily and quietly slide up the deck. He always carried well-maintained chains and straps that were long enough for any sized tire or vehicle. His truck was the pride of my fleet because he always kept his hands clean by wearing gloves and wiping his hands after every repossession. He had all the right tools and "all the right moves" to always get the job done.

What was the difference between Ron and my other agents? I will admit that the fault was mine. The fact that my other agents were not as good as Ron was actually my fault. I enjoyed spending time with Ron. It was not that I did not like being with the other agents, but Ron and I had a special relationship. We both had type A personalities, which would cause most people to guess that we would have clashed. Don't get me wrong, it wasn't all chocolates and hearts between us! We battled on more than one occasion and did not always agree. However, we both had many things in common—the same sense of humor, the same goal of building a giant company, and the same values regarding professionalism and standards. We were closer in age, had the same work ethic (workaholics!), and liked earning a lot of money. We could work 24 hours straight, and we were always willing to stay up and go after "just one more car."

I appreciated what he did for the company, how he maintained his equipment, and to be honest, that he was a company man! We were probably more like family or brothers than an employer and an employee.

For all of these reasons, I tended to gravitate toward spending time with him, sharing my knowledge, and mentoring him. If he called me at 3:00 a.m. needing my expertise on a job, I threw on my boots and work clothes and ran out the door like a fireman going to a 3:00 a.m. fire.

Again, I admit, my other agents were not better than they were because of me. They were all good, but they could have been better—a whole lot better. That would have made them more money and me more money. I would spend some time with the others, but not nearly the amount of time that I should have. Quite possibly, the quality of time and the level of mentorship I gave was much less than what I gave Ron. If I had it to do all over again, I would have spread my mentorship and time around more evenly among all of my repossessors.

Meet with Your Agents as Often as Possible

I was supposed to meet with a repossession company owner to evaluate some practices he had instituted with his business. I suggested meeting for breakfast or lunch, and he replied, "How about 9:30 p.m. at my office?" Normally, even if I travel to another state and stay in a hotel, my consulting business hours are 9:00 a.m. to 5:00 p.m. I pulled all those late nights for years, and I now enjoy working days! However, I really cared about this owner and his company, so I came to his office at 9:30 p.m. as he had requested.

When I saw what he was doing, I immediately wished I had done something similar. His wife and father ran the business during the day, and he was also there for part of the day. But he made sure he was there at 9:30 p.m. to check with his drivers, go over accounts, listen to their complaints, and inspect their equipment.

He had a large screen television on the wall with Clearplan displayed so he could go over older accounts with them to see if they were missing anything or if he could help in any way. He offered them tips, corrected them if necessary, and even elected to jump in a wrecker with them and spend the night or half of the night riding with them. He was also able to monitor when they started their shift by being there at that time. He would also meet with his camera car drivers and get them set up in zones and lay out what he wanted them to do and where he wanted them to go that night. The only perk I might have added was to have a pot of hot coffee brewing for the agents for when they walked in the door. But then again, what do I know? I was rarely at my office at that time of night to meet with my guys. But if I had to do it all over again, I certainly would do exactly what he was doing.

AGENTS MUST COMPLETE THEIR UPDATES

Make sure your agents update their accounts properly and know why they are doing so.

I have already addressed updates and how important they are to the client. However, the repo company owner, the spotter/camera car driver and the repo agent are three others who also benefit from good updates.

What do agents hate the most? Updates! No one likes being a pencil pusher! It's always more exciting to repo cars! Nothing interrupts the repossession agent's sleep more than the office staff calling because an update is needed and wasn't done. I also hate updates with a passion. I discovered the way to avoid doing updates was to make sure I picked up the collateral!

One of the common complaints I hear from clients and repo company owners is the failure to receive accurate and timely account updates from the repossession agents. The reasons include accounts not being updated often enough, unclear information, or poor spelling and grammar usage on the reports. The updates a client receives provide a snapshot of what your company represents. Make sure you train your agents and employees on how to do them right. Instruct them to take the extra minute to be thorough with their update and to go back and proofread before submitting it.

If your agents are clueless about the importance of updates, explain it to them. Let them know that an update can be viewed by the client as a matter that is equally as important as the collateral being picked up. An average account update done often enough shows them that you are at least working the order. Updates containing multiple details or more info than other companies' agents provide shows your company is working that account hard. Hard work is what the lender wants, and working hard will earn a company a great reputation. This results in the client's issuing you more orders. If the performance of all of your agents netted you 10 or 20 more orders issued for your company every month, imagine the increased revenue and profit!

Updates Are Important for the Agent

Besides being important to the clients, account updates are beneficial for the agents as well. Agents are running an overwhelming number of repossessions, and remembering what they have and have not done on each account can be difficult. Each night the agent should go over his updates before he begins to run his accounts. That way he knows what he has to do that night to get accounts picked up. As he is reading his updates, he may see something that he has overlooked. Agents work long hours and are often mentally fatigued. Having and reviewing the update will help them to stay focused on the next step to get the job done.

For the Camera Car Driver/Spotter

The Camera Car Driver/Spotter's providing good updates can be invaluable to everyone. It can show that the account is being run frequently, validate an update that the agent already gave, or invalidate an update the agent gave. The agent is probably not lying or giving phony updates.

I followed my GPS to an address one night, described an address, and the very next night, the GPS took me to a house a few doors away. Besides the fact that a GPS can be incorrect, I had also misread the address on the first night. Mistakes happen, and fortunately those mistakes can be caught by having the Camera Car Driver/Spotter provide a confirmation update.

Updates Are Important
for the Repo Company Owner/Manager

The manager of the repossession company can look at updates and ensure that all the bases have been covered by the agent. By reviewing the agent's actions, he can determine if something has been missed. Perhaps the agent is not thoroughly running the account. He may only be checking on the midnight or afternoon shift and not running the account during the day. Possibly he has not actually knocked on the door of the account or checked the debtor's place of employment. Once the manager has determined that all the bases have been covered, he can decide if some in-house skip tracing needs to be done. The account may need to be reassigned to an agent who runs accounts more aggressively.

SCHEDULING

One mistake I believe I made was allowing my agents to work the hours and shifts they needed to get the job done. Of course, they sometimes had to run on midnights to hit all of the home addresses properly. But I left the decision of when they ran days and afternoons to their discretion. Often, because of sleep or family conflicts, those two shifts would sometimes be neglected. As soon as I picked up on that neglect becoming a problem, I found myself putting the hammer down and insisting that they hit those two shifts.

If I had to do it all over again, I believe I would have had my agents work six days a week with Saturdays as their off night. I would have them run Sunday midnights and bounce back on Monday around 7:00 p.m. until around 4:00 a.m. on Tuesday so they could hit the evening time and into the midnight shift. After that, the shift would begin bright and early on Wednesday at around 3:00 a.m. and run until about noon to hit the early mornings and day shift for POE's. Then the next shift start time would be around 10:00 p.m. until around 8:00 a.m. on Thursday morning. I would schedule their last night with a 2:00 a.m. start time on Friday until around noon Saturday morning.

With those wreckers out working, I would couple them with camera car driver/spotters out working. I would have them grid zones and also spot addresses from repossession orders. I would coordinate where they ran with the agents so the agents would be close enough to go repo a plate hit. But I would have the repossessors running accounts exactly opposite to the areas the spotters were running so the addresses could be checked at different times. I would encourage the agents and the spotters to communicate and alter the running of addresses, depending on time, distance and whether or not the agent was tied up running a car back to the lot that was either a regular repo or a plate hit.

During the daytime, I would have a repossession agent (or more than one) working along with the appropriate number of camera cars that the agent(s) could handle. The repossessor could be picking up voluntaries and also be available to pick up a plate hit by the camera car. The camera car and the repossessor could also run POE's and other addresses on day shift.

Your scheduling should be detailed so agents and camera car drivers are not running the same accounts or areas. Scheduling should also depend on your repossession assignment volume, work area, and staffing. My suggestions are only suggestions, so tailor your scheduling to what works for you.

TAKING HOME WRECKERS VS. SHARING

When I owned my company, I allowed my agents to take their wreckers home. The deal I had with them was that they would be on call for needed pickups. I found that many of my agents were frequently unavailable for those call outs, and when this happened, I reversed my methodology. (Again, how you handle this situation is up to you!)

My thought was that an agent would take better care of *his* wrecker if it were *his,* but experience has not always proven this to be true. I also thought that by sharing trucks, agents would pass the blame for any damage to the person with whom they shared a truck. The blame game can easily be minimized by having the agents always complete a wrecker inspection form at the beginning of their shift. If damage is found, they are to note and email time-stamped photos to the owner or manager.

One of the main concerns I had that caused me to change my position on taking home wreckers was company equipment sitting unused for nearly eight hours a day while the agent was sleeping. The agent's personal and family time probably bumped that down time to 12 or 13 hours. For a company owning 5 wreckers, that downtime represents 65 hours every day. In a six-day work week, those wreckers are sitting idle for 390 hours. What a waste of equipment! The company could put two clean-up crews together on the agent's day off, running for 24 hours straight. That clean-up day, plus the 390 hours of down time, adds up to a multitude of cars that could be repossessed with those trucks.

Additionally, those wreckers' being used for personal use incurred fuel costs. The possibility of a wrecker's being vandalized while sitting at an agent's house was always a possibility. An unhappy debtor's seeing the wrecker and knowing where an agent lived could be dangerous for both the agent and his family.

MAKE SURE YOUR AGENTS HAVE THE RIGHT TOOLS

The following is a fairly comprehensive list of everything I believe every repossessor needs to possess to function well at his job.

1) **A mechanically sound wrecker.** You will want a clean and dependable wrecker. You will look like a fool if you break down in someone's driveway while you are trying to snag his ride. A self-loader would be my first recommendation, but if you can get the job done with a wrecker with an "L" arm system, then go for it. I was using one long before self-loaders came on the scene and repossessed as many cars back then as I can with a self-loader. For your wreckers, you will need a hot spot or air card for mobile Internet, gas cards for agents to fuel the trucks, and an organized insurance and vehicle registration packet.

2) **A reliable flashlight.** You need one that always works by having either a fresh set of batteries on hand or a mounted, on-board charging system. It can be quite windy in the middle of the night, and using a Bic lighter to read a VIN screams, "I'm a hobo." After all, I saw an agent try it once!

3) **A Global Positioning System (GPS).** When I first started working as a repossession agent, I had to carry dozens of paper maps for every city I worked in. Thank goodness, with the advancement of technology, repossessors do not have to use them any longer. Whether it is a stand-alone unit or an app on the agent's phone, this tool is a must for saving time and money. I recently traveled the country on a three-month vacation and found my cell phone's GPS to be quite accurate. It was never wrong when it announced that I had arrived and told me if the address was on the left or right. I only had one problem when I was traveling on a newly constructed road that had recently opened.

4) **An organizer for repossession orders and other paperwork.** Of course, in this day and age of computers, workflow systems, Clearplan, and other advanced technology, file folders and paper files are seemingly obsolete. However, an agent may often be confronted by a debtor who wants to see the repossession order for himself. What should the agent do when that happens? Allow the debtor to climb into his wrecker and look at the order on his laptop screen?! At times the hard copy of the repossession order is most effective.

5) **A laptop with a laptop stand.** A laptop is necessary for updating and checking emails, using Clearplan, accessing the LPT camera system the company uses, as well as having Internet

access in the field. The laptop stand will save you the cost of replacing your laptop because you had to brake suddenly to avoid hitting a squirrel or other road obstruction. Only a few things are worse than seeing your unsecured laptop go flying off your passenger seat and smashing down on your floorboard.

6) **A wedge, a stick, and a door pump.** The days of the 300-piece breakout kit are nearly over. If you do not have these three items, then you need to go directly to a local or online supplier and make that purchase.

7) **A wide variety of high quality chain lengths, "J" hooks, tow straps and ratchets specifically designed for the wrecker the agent is using.** You need to have the right lengths and sizes to tow any size tire or vehicle. You don't want to see the monster truck you repossessed go skidding past you because you did not have tow straps long enough to strap it down. Trust me, if this happens, it will take less than a minute for your client to delete you off his "preferred" agent list forever. You should also have some straps to tie off a steering wheel that won't lock. Yes, I know that you usually use the seat belt for that, but what if the seat belt is missing or can't be pulled out?

8) **An air tank.** Fix-a-flat and a plug-in-the-cigarette-lighter type tire pump may be cheap and easy to store, but they are notoriously unreliable. An air tank is the most reliable tool you can have in your truck to inflate the tires on your debtor's vehicle.

9) **Jumper cables or a portable jump-start pack.** You will come across a slew of dead batteries in the auto repossession business, so you will need jumper cables or a portable jump-start pack.

10)   **Mechanic's tools.** Have an assortment of sockets, ratchets, screw drivers, crescent wrenches, and regular wrenches. You never know what you will need out there.

11)   **High quality tow dollies.**

12)   **A motorcycle attachment.** Always keep it in your wrecker in case you locate a motorcycle you have been looking for. I remember learning this lesson when I got a call from a debtor who had been telling me for three months he was never giving up his Harley. I answered, and he told me he wanted me to come get his cycle right away. I was ten minutes from where the bike was but two hours from the shop, where my motorcycle attachment was sitting on a shelf. That instance of forgetfulness added four unnecessary hours to my day!

THE REPO MAN'S PERSONAL TOOLS TO GET THROUGH THE NIGHT

(a) **Gloves, hand cleaner, baby wipes, and some clean towels.** Cleanliness is next to godliness, and a grease-free wrecker interior also means more dollars in your pocket when you later sell it. I have to mention that your truck is your office, and you will be more productive if it is clean and neat.

(b) **Clean clothes, steel toe work boots, some breath mints or gum, and maybe a spare deodorant and bottle of cologne for those long hours.** I know the public perceives the repo man as a stinky grease ball, but we don't have to fit the image.

(c) **An assortment of snacks, beverages, and your favorite tunes on CD to make the night enjoyable.**

My last list of recommendations includes a high quality

ballistic vest, brains, street smarts, and the decision-making ability to know when it is time to call it a night. Most repo-men have a family to go home to, so develop a sixth sense to identify a situation that is unsafe or might even turn deadly. Driving off on your own free will and volition rather than being carted off in an ambulance is always the best choice.

I carried a lot of extras in my wrecker that I called "two-for's," meaning I carried two of most everything for when something got broken or lost. This included extra gloves, hats, clothing, screws, bolts, nuts, cotter pins, ink pens, WD-40, ratchets, straps, and anything else I could think of.

AGENTS AND THE OFFICE

One last note on the relationship between the office staff and the field agents: sometimes a disconnect occurs between the office staff and the field agents. Both need to understand that one cannot get the job done without the other. You need to ensure that your agents understand the amount of work and pressure that the office is under every day. Make sure the agents know that treating the office staff politely when they interact with them is important.

I recently spent some time with one repo company owner whose company was plagued with low morale and employee conflicts. So much strife was taking place between all of his staff that I can only describe the office as a toxic, hostile work environment. I advised him to address the issues immediately, put all employees involved on a 90-day performance improvement plan (PIP), and review the PIP's every 30 days.

I told the owner that he needed to put the troublemakers on notice, telling them that if they did not fix their issues, they would be let go.

The owner basically informed me that he did not have the time nor the desire to be a babysitter and that his staff needed to work out their issues. I explained to him that nothing was going to be made right by ignoring the problem. I warned him that he needed to take a leadership role immediately—before the "powder keg cooking over a high flame exploded."

The owner chose to do nothing, and within a matter of weeks, one agent assaulted another one with a deadly weapon. In the ensuing brawl, both agents ended up in the emergency room. The incident not only put two agents out of commission for a few weeks, but word of the incident filtered out to some of the company's clients, and the repo company lost work over the owner's refusal to take responsibility for an unfortunate work environment.

I cannot stress the importance of agents, office staff, managers, and owners who work together to maintain a pleasant atmosphere in the work environment.

CHAPTER ELEVEN

"Gather 'round, boys.
It's time for our weekly certification class."

Training and Career Development

THE OTHER DAY I was conversing with a repo company owner. While we were sitting in his office chatting, we were also watching a twenty-something young man working in the company storage lot. I noticed that he seemed to be a hard worker and was getting a lot done in the short time we were watching him. I mentioned how hard he was working to the owner who responded, "He's a great worker. He's dependable, does everything he's told to do, and is probably the best employee I've ever had."

"Why don't you have him in a wrecker repossessing cars?"

The owner shook his head as he said, "The kid does not see repossessing cars as a *real* career."

As I was leaving, my path happened to cross with that of the young man, and I struck up a conversation with him. In our talking, I asked him if he had ever thought about moving up in the company and becoming a repossession agent one day. Just like the owner had told me, he replied, "I feel that being a repossessor is not a real career." Before I could respond, he added, "I wasn't trying to be disrespectful, but these guys are all cowboys. There is no real training or standards, and everyone does what he wants. The repo business is weird, the agents come and go—even if they make big money. And the owner is frustrated because he cannot teach them anything. They all feel like they know everything already."

What a mouthful! That young man certainly had a lot of insight for being a storage lot worker! How sad that someone with his work ethic would not see a being a repossession agent as a career. Why? Is it because the industry has been allowed to remain stagnant without growing by professionalizing how the business operates?

I know many agents who earn between $60,000 and $100,000 a year. I would argue that if someone is paid that well, then he ought to be held to some sort of standard. I would also wager that those making less than those figures could likely hit those numbers if they were trained and mentored properly.

What would that mean for the repossession industry as a whole? Happier, well-paid agents; higher profits for repo company owners; more cars picked up, leading to happier clients with fewer financial losses; and fewer on-the-job injuries, insurance claims, lawsuits, and fines. Training and mentoring in this industry would certainly be worth it with those results!

WHY TAKE AUTO REPOSSESSION TRAINING?

Employees of the creditor, forwarders, auto repossession companies, and repossession agents are all taking some sort of yearly training. Have you ever wondered why you are doing so? I think most readers have answered that question in their mind, but theirs may be uninformed answers. Was your answer, "To get a certificate"? Or maybe, "Because a vendor manager told me I had to"? A reason often heard is "If the training isn't taken, work from a certain client will be discontinued."

Is that a good reason for training? Only if you think going to college just to get a diploma is a good reason! Or maybe you'd choose a surgeon to perform lifesaving surgery on you solely based on his receiving a diploma. Wouldn't it matter more if the doctor actually gained an extensive amount of knowledge in medical school? Would you want a mechanic working on your wrecker who only worried about getting a certificate? Or one who actually learned everything about how to repair vehicles? Your first choice in retaining a lawyer to represent you in a divorce would be the one who learned the most about divorce law—not the one who managed to get his law diploma just so he could get more clients. The person who has the most knowledge is always the best choice in any decision. So why, in the auto repossession industry, is a training certificate more important than the knowledge learned?

More than a certificate, there should be one main reason for taking auto repossession training—to save the creditors, forwarders, insurance companies, and auto repossession companies money. How can that be? They have to pay for training, so it is an expense—not a savings. Right? Wrong! Actually, the money spent is greatly outweighed by the money saved. The savings is realized by minimizing employee turnover, reducing risks, and producing better managers and repossession agents. Money is saved in an even more effective way when an entire industry is professionalized by training and standards. The benefits that result are immeasurable and not just monetarily. The larger payoff will be seen in the quality of company environments that develop and how the auto repossession industry, as a whole, will be viewed by government agencies and the general public.

CHANGING AN ENTIRE INDUSTRY
FOR THE BETTER THROUGH TRAINING AND MENTORING

For some reason, auto repossession sees itself as being different than any other business in the world. In a way it is different—at least when it comes to the job that is being performed. No other business focuses on peeling someone's car off their driveway because that person hit a financial bump in the road! But nonetheless, it is still a business.

In some ways, the repossession industry is stuck in the 1950s, with no formal standards, safety practices, training or continuing education, or other process that other industries put in place to make improvements. From most of the clients to the repossession company owner to the repossession agent to the government, no real standards exist. Oil refineries are subject to regulations, safety standards, and required training, and the companies pass those same standards on to their employees and contractors. Name any other occupation—nurses, doctors, steel workers, school teachers, truck drivers, cab drivers, etc.—and a handbook of standards, safety practices, training or CEUs will be given to the employee.

Yet the repossession industry, as dangerous as it can be, seems to have none of that. Since no one is requiring it, I recommend that the individual repossession owners step up and fill in that gap. Again, doing so will reduce injury, death, lawsuits, fines, and other risks for everyone from the lender down to the person working in the office or storage lot.

No wonder the profits in the repossession industry are not so much higher. Every business needs to constantly be bettering itself and its industry. The repo business needs to constantly be evaluating process, procedures, and standards and raising the bar higher when a gap is identified. What other industry stagnates and stalls in professionalism and pay? Could the repossession industry as a whole be standing still at lower fees in this century than they were when I got into this business in 1988? If so, I dare say the impasse is due in great part because the industry has not grown much in professionalism.

Sure, a few states have enacted licensing requirements along with some mandatory training. But why are owners waiting for a state that knows absolutely nothing about the auto repossession industry to set up standards and laws? Why are repossession companies not policing themselves with training and standards?

TRAINING

Every repossession company should have training for their employees, including new hire orientation, written and online training, on-the-job training, continuing education, practical hands-on training, and safety training. The owners and managers should take training on leadership, business-related skills, and other subjects that will help them be better owners and managers.

Training should be provided in the following areas (and probably in more areas):

- Federal, state, and local laws that pertain to the auto repossession industry
- Defensive driving
- Safe towing procedures
- Safety training in every area that pertains to the environment in which employees work. This training could include anything from safe walking in the snow to driving in foggy conditions to how to lift heavy items safely.
- Cyber security
- Leadership. Every manager or business owner can always benefit from leadership training.
- Business ethics
- Sexual harassment. With every other industry instituting mandatory training on sexual harassment, why doesn't the repossession industry follow suit?
- Cultural diversity is addressed in every other business, yet the repossession industry has never thought to see the importance of instituting training.
- Customer service. In all sincerity, I have called some repossession companies with atrocious customer service. Why this industry seems to feel the need to be unpleasant to callers is beyond me. Because the business is composed of tough guys, and so are the men and women working the phones?!

- Active shooter training for situations that arise with angry people on a daily basis. I am somewhat surprised that an active shooter scenario has not taken place at a repo agency. All that is needed is one angry debtor attempting to retaliate with violence against the company responsible for repossessing his car.

- Career development teaches how to effectively evaluate your staff, utilize performance improvement plans, and properly conduct an internal investigation. The tools learned in the material will help you to better develop your staff without having to fire and hire so often. This will lead to more productivity and professionalism, as well as extending employee retention.

- Practical skip tracing covers practical and easy ways to find debtors utilizing free (or low cost) resources and includes real-life case studies. Imagine how much more profitable you would be if you used this knowledge to find 5, 10, 20 or more pieces of collateral every week!

- Successful employee engagement training in the auto repossession industry can be the solution to what seems to be a revolving door of employee turnover when it comes to your agents and office staff. Successfully engaging an employee is more than just a "hello" in the yard or a five-minute phone call about an account. It begins with recruiting talent and includes the onboarding of a new employee, making sure the employee stays motivated, ensuring he is recognized for positive behavior, and finally, as a last resort, the employee's termination. There are proper ways in handling each one of these areas that lead to successful employee engagement.

▪ Repossessor safety moments messages can greatly reduce injury, accidents, and civil liability in your organization.

Revolutionary ideas? Not really for most businesses; however, importance being placed on these types of training topics seems to be scarce in the repo industry. The repossession world invests in wreckers, rollbacks, LPR camera systems, camera cars, computers, other office equipment, and more. How much is being invested in the career development of the repossession agents and employees? I believe this one neglected business investment will pay off in a great way!

As the old saying goes, knowledge is power, and training is a powerful necessity that the repossession industry is in dire need of instituting. Training, education, personal mentorship, and career development help to better an employee in many areas that will prove positive for your company—bringing up profits and reducing incidents of risk such as lawsuits, crashes, fines, loss of clients, and damage to the business's reputation.

Operations Manual

Every repossession agency should have an operations manual that details every procedure, rule, process and consequence for not following the manual. All employees should receive a copy, be required to read it within an assigned time period, and then sign the agreement to follow the rules.

The manual should detail everything, including sick and vacation days, days-off requirements, sexual harassment, internal investigations, how to talk to a debtor, safety procedures, and anything pertinent to the business. This manual should not be a dusty book on a shelf that is covered in cobwebs. The manual should be used, followed, constantly reviewed, and updated as needed. It should be the only guideline that everyone uniformly follows. The standard operating procedure (SOP) should be used to mete out all disciplinary issues and guidance to every employee.

CAREER DEVELOPMENT

Repossession company owners and their managers ought to be developing their employees into something better at all times. Continual and constant improvement should be the goal. Owners and managers should conduct quarterly and yearly written employee evaluations. When agents and employees are lacking in certain areas, constructively discuss the matter with them. Do not yell, curse, scream, or berate them! The job of an owner and a manager is to positively influence his employees to be better, and destroying their morale with those kinds of negative actions will not achieve that goal.

CONDUCT ANNUAL PERFORMANCE REVIEWS

Sit down with your employees and go over a written performance review on their job performance with them. Let them list what they think their strengths and weaknesses are. Discuss where you think their performance is over and above, right on target, and lacking. Give powerful kudos and positives to build them up and soften the negatives. Use the negatives in a way that shows your desire to help rather than being critical.

Use Performance Improvement Plans (PIPs) to set out 90-day goals of improvement in areas where they are under-performing. Meet with them every 30 days to gauge improvement or the lack thereof.

CHAPTER TWELVE

"I am here for my personal property...
uhhhh, you can keep my wife."

STORAGE LOT AND PERSONAL PROPERTY MANAGEMENT

STORAGE LOT SECURITY

YOUR STORAGE LOT needs to be as secure as possible. Adequate fencing, topped with barbed wire, should be present as a preventive measure to break-ins and theft. Dusk-to- dawn lighting is also a must, and I would suggest investing an extensive video surveillance system as well. Strategically install cameras around the lot and in any buildings that you wish to monitor. Find a surveillance system that has a feature to view remotely from a phone, iPad or other computer. Having cameras with motion detection that alert your phone and email are another feature you should consider.

I would also post signs stating "the property is under video surveillance," "beware of dog, and "no trespassing." Of course, most insurance companies prohibit guard dogs on the premises; the bad guys won't know whether or not you have one. All of these signs will make them think twice about breaking in.

I used the tried and tested padlocked chain around my gate; however, a chain can be easily cut and a padlock smashed open with little effort. If I owned a repossession company today, I would install an electric gate that could be opened with a remote fob or a code that can be issued to your staff. This type of gate eliminates issuing gate keys to employees. Each employee would be assigned his own unique code that can be cancelled if he leaves the company. The owner can also track who comes and goes in the storage lot. If you have an employee theft problem, you can pinpoint when particular staff members were at the property versus when the theft occurred.

Organizing your Storage Lot

When I owned my repo company, I had a staging area that was utilized for new repossessions to be entered. The agent bringing in the car had to write the following on the driver's side front window with a grease pen:

- The name of the lender
- The loan account number
- The date the collateral was repossessed
- The letter K with a circle around it if the collateral had keys with it. If it did not come with keys, then the agent just wrote the letter K with no circle on it.

The agents also placed small orange cones on top of the vehicles dropped in this staging area. The orange cone could not be removed until the following conditions were met:

- Personal property had been removed, labeled and properly stored.
- Keys were made (or obtained by the customer) if required by the client.

- Mileage was noted on the condition report.
- Condition report was 100 percent complete.
- Photographs of the vehicle were taken from all angles.

Once those conditions were all met, the vehicle was then moved to an area that identified collateral stored there as ready to be delivered to auction or ready to be picked up by a transport company.

Another area in my storage lot was designated for long-term storage or for collateral that the client identified as ones that we needed to hold so the debtor could come to our lot and redeem their vehicle.

You can consider utilizing a variety of other staging areas, which can be divided by any of the following categories:

- All-wheel drive vehicles in one area so other vehicles are not blocked in while keys are being made
- Wrecked or non-running vehicles to prevent blocking in other pieces of collateral
- Oversized vehicles or other specialized pieces of collateral
- By client/lender
- Indoor storage for motorcycles, ATVs and other collateral that the clients want shielded from the elements.

Storage Fees

Some clients allow for daily storage fees to be charged while you store their collateral at your lot. Others request ten days free, while some others want unlimited free storage. If you can charge a storage fee, then do so. Every little bit of revenue counts toward the bigger picture of your repo company's profitability. If you have a large boat, RV, or camper that takes up several spaces and the lender will pay it, charge an oversized storage fee.

Condition Reports

Some repo companies have the agents who picked up the car do their own condition reports, and others have their lot staff do all of the condition reports. I went with the latter for two reasons:

1) I wanted my agents in and out of my lot as quickly as possible. They made money when they picked up cars—not when tied up doing paperwork.

2) I wanted condition reports done during daylight hours so damage would not be missed because of poor lighting. Missing a scratch or a dent not caused by your recovery of the vehicle means you will most likely be paying for repairs if the debtor complains. If damage is missed on the condition report, then your defense is also missing.

Again, how you handle condition reports is entirely up to you.

Whatever decision you make, be sure that your reports are accurate and detailed. I never put "excellent condition" on any condition report. A vehicle cannot be in excellent condition unless it is rolling off the assembly line or sitting in a new car dealer showroom. And if you look carefully enough, even some of the cars that are sitting in the showroom may have a blemish or two!

Personal Property

Repossession companies have to be extremely careful when dealing with personal property that is found in the collateral that they recover. If property is mishandled, damaged or lost, your company might be responsible for paying a replacement fee to the debtor. Make sure that you follow your state laws as well as the lender's contractual agreement with you when it comes to personal property.

Personal property includes personal effects that are found in the collateral that belong to the debtor or someone that he knows. It is not anything that has been affixed to the collateral, such as after-market rims, a replacement stereo system, speaker or other items that are bolted down.

A good rule of thumb for determining whether or not an item is personal property that the debtor can have is that if the item is worth something to him and can be removed from the vehicle without using tools, the debtor may have the item. Of course, this does not include stock floormats or the spare tire in the trunk!

You will need to do a detailed inventory of all personal property found in the vehicle. When you inventory property, be especially detailed when listing items. Count all money and list the exact amount. If you list "some cash" when only $28 was found in the vehicle, the debtor can claim that $500 was missing. An accurate amount noted in the personal property inventory is your best defense. List the exact number of CDs and any other items left in the vehicle.

Gold, Diamonds, and Other Shiny Stuff

When listing jewelry, make sure you realize you are not a certified jeweler. If you list "big diamond ring" and it is a fake stone, the debtor may claim that his real diamond ring is missing and demand repayment. Use terms like "gold color" or the name or a watch followed by "authenticity unknown," i.e., "Rolex, authenticity unknown."

Labeling and Storing Personal Property

Place all of the personal effects found in a cardboard box and label the box with the debtor's name, the lender, and the date that the vehicle was recovered. Also put the date that the property can be disposed of on the box as well. You should have a room, a semi-trailer, a shipping container, or even an old school bus in which to store the property. I used an old school bus that I purchased for $100 and was able to store property alphabetically by labeling the seats with letters. You can build a shelving system inside any of the above options to organize all personal property. Whatever you use to store your property, make sure the place is dry and secure. Of course, large amounts of cash or valuable jewelry needs to be stored in a more secure area such a safe.

Bag and Tag Fees

If the client allows it, charge a bag and tag fee. Someone from your company cleaned out that collateral, professionally detailed the property, placed it in secure box, tagged it, and then moved the box to your secure property storage area. You had to pay someone to complete this task, so if possible, try to be compensated for the work.

Documentation and Secure Storage Will Protect You

To avoid problems with personal property, I recommend that you keep it longer than what is required. If you are required to keep it 60 days, then store it 120 days. Send the debtor a certified letter informing him that you have property that was in the vehicle you repossessed. In the letter, you should state that you are only keeping the property for as long as the state requires and list the date that the items will be disposed of or donated to charity. Even then, store the belongings longer because debtors always show up to get their "important" papers or valuables the day after their belongings were donated to Goodwill. I had people who called me two years after recovering their vehicle, expecting us to still have their property!

I know of some repo companies that were very sloppy with personal property, and that disorganization cost them money. When debtors redeem personal property, make a written record. The debtor should be the only person allowed to redeem property—not parents, boyfriend, friend, or anyone else. The debtor needs to come in, present either a state ID or a driver's license in order to receive his property. Once his identity confirms he is the debtor, he needs to sign a dated document that he received his property. The document should list all of the property that was inventoried and boxed. Keeping detailed documents will prevent people from making false claims of lost or stolen property and will help prevent your company from paying a settlement in the event of a lawsuit.

Once you are past the date that you are required to keep the debtor's property, then you may donate it to charity. Make sure you obtain a receipt from the charitable organization that received the donated items. This receipt will serve as documentation of how you disposed of the property and could be used as a possible tax write-off for your company.

HAZMAT, CHEMICALS AND LIQUIDS

Consider implementing a policy about not storing liquids. Storing gasoline and other flammable liquids can be a fire hazard. Another issue of consideration may be storing a variety of unknown liquids that could be spilled. Certain chemicals mixed together could cause an explosion and a resulting fire or release poisonous gases and other HAZMAT dangers that could be detrimental to you, your staff, or the surrounding community.

CHAPTER THIRTEEN

"Maybe I can use these LPR cameras
to webcam chat with girls on the Internet
or what?"

SKIP TRACING

SKIP TRACING IS no longer needed. Really? I beg to differ with you!

I recently heard the following from a repossession agent: "We don't need no stinkin' skip tracers; we got LPR cameras, and they find everything."

LPR cameras are great and one of the best tools the industry has ever had, but they are not the end all to finding every piece of collateral. LPR camera cars do not often hit rural areas, and sometimes they are not able to get into certain areas, like gated communities, parking garages, and other places that prohibit access. They are also random, and luck plays a huge part in getting a hit on the plate of a vehicle that is up for repossession. This industry still has a need for skip tracing from the client side to the repo company office to the front line repossessor who is working out in the field.

SKIP TRACING DEFINED

Skip tracing is "the process of utilizing a variety of tasks and techniques to locate a person's location." A *skip tracer* is "an individual who performs these tasks and techniques to locate a person." Skip tracers may be just that—a skip tracer. However, lawyers, police officers, news reporters and journalists, real estate agents and investors, repossession agents, private investigators, process servers, bail recovery agents, debt collectors, and other occupations often perform the skip-tracing work.

A *skip* is "the target person who is being sought by the skip tracer." The term *skip* came from the old adage "skipped town." This term was used and is still used to describe a person who quickly left the area to avoid something. A criminal might leave town to avoid being arrested for a crime he has committed. Sometimes, a gang member may take off because a rival gang has put a "hit" on him. A divorce may occur, and the ex-husband may relocate to another state to avoid paying child support or alimony. For the repossession world, a debtor may go into hiding to avoid having his vehicle repossessed.

How It is done

Skip tracing is accomplished by collecting and analyzing information about the individual being sought. The analysis process consists of taking all that information, breaking it down, and abbreviating it by pulling unsubstantiated data, leaving only the verified facts. Many times a current location for your skip can be found hidden in the massive amount of information compiled and sifted through.

Skip tracing involves the use of databases, credit reports, loan application information, criminal and civil background checks, and other information. Much of this information is available to the general public. Skip tracing also involves contacting former associates of the target to obtain and verify information to ascertain an accurate location for the skip.

Skip Tracing Legally

If you are going to learn how to skip trace properly, make sure you learn how to do it legally. Get a license if the state to are operating in requires you to be licensed. Learn the federal laws pertaining to skip tracing and everything about how the Federal Trade Commission (FTC), the Consumer Financial Protection Agency, and other federal regulators enforce these laws. Learn all about the Fair Debt Collection Practices Act (FDCPA), The Gramm-Leach Bliley Act (GLBA), the Fair Credit Reporting Act (FCRA), and the Driver's Privacy Protection Act (DPPA).

You Are Not Allowed to Skip Trace or Do Any Investigative Work

In today's world of auto repossessions, some clients forbid their repossession contractors from doing skip work. Some lenders still encourage and are even willing to pay for that investigative work. The benefit to doing some "pre-skip," which in the industry is sometimes referred to as a *light skip,* is that most of the methods you use are free, so there is no cost to your business. Doing some freebies that do not take too much time may uncover an unknown address and pull some extra cash into your repossession business that the original repossession order information would not have.

I assigned a staff member in my office to routinely pre-skip every involuntary repossession issued to my company. I felt this person's work was invaluable and worth the money to take on the task of uncovering new information. That work was for my repo agents who got the collateral picked up on the first run of the account.

FREE SKIPPING

Because it does not cost anything, the best skip tracing can be done online using sites like Facebook, Twitter, Instagram, and other websites. Learn how to utilize free online record searches of databases on property records, marriage licenses, voter records, and occupational licensing.

The Internet is simply a tool. Understand that the Internet cannot locate skips, but talented skip tracers who know how to analyze data do.

CHAPTER FOURTEEN

High gas prices never bother the owner
of Cheapo Repo Co. What's his secret?!

Running Lean

Looking at the Cost of Business

THE AUTO REPOSSESSION business is by no means a cheap business in which to be involved. Many costs immediately come to my mind, and then there are some additional costs that you really have to think to come up with. Those costs tend to add up quicker than you think. If you are going to be in this business, you need to find ways to keep costs down and shop around for the best deals on everything.

Wreckers, Trucks and Equipment

One of the largest expenditures in the auto repossession business is your wrecker. The prices for wreckers have shot up year after year, and unfortunately, the pay per repossession has not risen much. You are looking at spending around $65,000-plus for a brand-new self-loader. Decide in advance whether or not you plan to buy a new or a used wrecker. The new truck will cost more per month, but a used truck may break down often and be costly to maintain and repair. Don't forget that along with the cost of your new truck, you will also be paying a hefty insurance bill to cover your new investment.

You should also be sure to look at the different types of

trucks available. You could purchase a truck with a wrecker body, one with a slide-in unit, or one with a stinger. Some of those options are less expensive. Make sure you are aware of the tow limits of the truck you are considering, as well as the state requirements for the different types of trucks.

Another option that causes the price of a wrecker to go up or down is choosing a truck that has a gas engine over a diesel engine. Diesel will automatically be more expensive, but with proper maintenance, the diesel will last longer. A diesel wrecker will also get better gas mileage. One negative I can think of immediately is that diesel is currently more expensive per gallon. You will never know where fuel prices are going to go—up or down!

For years, I have heard that diesels are no good for repossession work. "They are too noisy, and the whole neighborhood will hear you coming," the so-called "connoisseurs" say. The diesel engines of today have overcome the disadvantages of being noisier and having maintenance issues. Now they are very quiet and require much less maintenance when compared to similar-sized gas engines.

I never found that a diesel wrecker hurt my repossession success at all—not even back in the day of the clattering, noisy diesels that existed back then. Because diesel motors are super tough and reliable, I prefer them over gas-powered trucks as my preference, based on my personal experiences of the years. However, this choice will be up to you and might come down to your personal preference, finances, or other factors.

REPOSSESSION AND OTHER INSURANCE

Repossession insurance costs are through the roof, and if you want to have a repossession business, then you will pay for it. Your coverage will have to include at the least a one-million-dollar general liability policy with wrongful repossession insurance, and a one-million-dollar aggregate vehicle liability policy for repossessions. This coverage cannot be just a tow policy because there is a difference. Other coverage may or may not be needed, depending on the lenders for whom you work. This could include insurance for your storage lot and people's personal property, workman's compensation, on-hook towing coverage, drive-away insurance, a million dollar per occurrence policy, and a dishonesty bond. You can be looking at paying several thousands of dollars a year for this coverage.

Like any other service for which you pay, you will want to shop around to find the best deal. Make sure the insurance companies match in rating and coverage. You may think you are getting a deal on repo insurance, only to find out that all you have is an insurance policy declaration page, but the insurance company's coverage and customer service are worthless.

LOCATION, LOCATION, LOCATION

*Weigh the Pros and Cons
When Choosing a Place to Hang Your Hat*

Another expense you will incur is for a storage lot and office rent. Make sure you shop around and find a safe and secure storage lot at a decent price. Whether you rent or finance the property, you will be paying this fee every month and not a onetime payment, so you will want to keep your costs down. When it comes to storage lot location versus cost, consider a few matters when shopping around for your storage yard.

THE RURAL LOCATION

You could rent a storage lot located in a rural area inexpensively. In fact, I once found a huge fenced-in lot in a little Amish farm town for around $200 a month. That fee even included a tiny office on the back of a building on the property and utilities! The only negative was that there was no bathroom—other than one at a service station a few blocks away. For $200 a month, you could drop a used storage container in the lot to use for property storage, rent a port-a-potty, operate your office from a cell phone, and use the same laptop in your wrecker and your office.

That sounds like a great price, right? Not so fast! First, you have to look at your service area. Would this location be so wonderful if a majority of your repossession orders are 45 minutes to an hour away from this lot location? That distance would add an extra one and a half-hour trip each time you had to tow only one piece of collateral there. If you repossessed four vehicles a night, that drive adds six long hours onto your already long night out. Still sound good? And don't forget the extra fuel expense, and the extra miles that will be racked up on your wrecker. The additional wear and tear to your equipment hasn't even been addressed.

Another factor to consider is the highways and roads to that location. During the winter months, snow removal is not as well maintained in rural areas. Sometimes the upkeep of rural roads is less than stellar, and some roads are not even blacktopped. Don't forget all the *uninsured* deer and other large animals that might dart in front of your wrecker, causing thousands of dollars of damage when you "road hunt" one of those critters!

Of course, you may be operating in a state that is nearly 100 percent rural, and none of these considerations matter. If that is the case, go with a rural or small-town location for your office and storage lot. If you are located in a predominantly rural state, make sure you are compensated by your clients for those cross-country collateral hunting expeditions.

THE MIDDLE OF THE CITY

Another option is to find an office and storage located right in the heart of the city in which you are working. You do not need to be downtown across from city hall unless you absolutely feel the need to see those town officials every day! However, a lot that is centrally located in the crosshairs of all your repo orders would be extremely convenient. You or your drivers could run out, grab a car a few minutes away, head back to the office, drop it at storage and head out to the next repo order! A whole lot less mileage would be put on your equipment, wear and tear would be nominal, and gas consumption would be much less. You might even bring in some extra revenue by getting on the city and county police towing rotation and doing vehicle relocation for some local businesses and apartment complexes.

This choice sounds like very lucrative place to set up shop, but there will certainly be some negatives to a big-city location. The rent or purchase price of such a location will be far more costly than the rural lot—even five, ten, twenty, or even a hundred times more expensive. I am certain that a repossession company storage lot in the middle of a big city like San Francisco will be closer to 100 times more expensive than other decent-sized cities like Indianapolis, Indiana; Detroit, Michigan; or Gary, Indiana. And in the cities I have listed, a location will be closer to ten or twenty times more expensive than an office and lot located in a rural area.

Being in a bigger city may also have some hidden costs, so check out how strict or how lax the city fathers are on their businesses. The city may have all sorts of ordinances about storing cars, business licensing, building safety and fire codes, handicapped parking and accessibility, etc. You certainly do not want to buy or rent a building in a city that has very expensive business requirements. You do not want to be installing a sprinkler system for fire safety, upgrading the electric on your building, doing asbestos cleanup, or being told you have to install an elevator to a second-floor office you will never use for a wheelchair-bound employee whom you do not employ! I do not want to sound callous, but you will need to consider every possible expense that could be assessed on your business.

THE SUBURBS OR THE EDGE OF TOWN

The next two sections will detail what I looked for before I even thought of renting a lot. I looked for a lot that was in between the towns and cities that comprised my major areas. Then the lot was centrally located for the majority of my repossession agents. The extra miles were eliminated on my wreckers, the gas usage was kept at a minimum, picking up property was convenient for the majority of debtors, and locating the place of business was easy for the transporters and vendors. For ease and convenience, I looked for a location that was close to my home, my bank, several filling stations that sold gas and diesel, auto part stores, a trusted mechanic, and some decent restaurants for grabbing lunch.

I also searched for a location that was close to as many major highways and toll roads as possible so I could quickly dispatch one of my employees via an express route to any location in my area for a repo or other tow. I also wanted my transporter rollbacks to be able to access a fast-moving highway as quickly as possible so they could be on their way to the auction and not caught in city traffic, stopping for stoplights every two blocks.

What if I Run in Both City and Rural Areas?

I ran in medium- to giant-sized cities as well as rural areas. I chose one pricier urban location for city storage, one medium-priced lot in a medium-sized town, and had some less expensive secure "drop" lots in rural areas. I insured all of my lots and made sure secure storage solutions were in place at all of them. My city drivers dropped off all of their collateral at a city lot in their area. My rural agents utilized the rural "drop" lots in their area, and my transporters (or a transport company) would make a run to the drop lots as often as needed to either transport collateral to one of my city lots or to one of the auto auctions we were required to use.

I allowed my rural drivers to keep bag and tag and storage fees that came in at one of those rural locations to compensate them for their time. They always appreciated the extra cash, and I was happy not to have to staff that rural lot with a lot boy who would normally handle those procedures.

A Crazy Expensive State or City

Another scenario you might be looking at is that you operate in a city that is super-expensive for renting or buying commercial property. You could consider locating in a suburb on the edge of that city's limits. To avoid these fees, I located right across the state line of one of the largest and most expensive cities in which I operated. Not only was the city out of sight expensive, so was the state. Gas was 15 percent to 25 percent higher, property taxes were ten to fifteen times higher, and so were sales, payroll and income taxes. My solution was to find a place right across the state line so I could save thousands upon thousands of dollars. Before you decide to make a decision like that, make sure that the state out of which you are moving will allow you to cross the state line to execute repossession and does not require your business to be located in that state.

So many monthly expenses arise in operating a repossession business, and I will try to address them all. There are gas, maintenance, and repair costs for every truck that you own. There will be the weekly salaries, taxes, and social security contributions for every one of your employees. Even if the banks are slow at paying you, your employees will still expect to receive their paychecks.

Initial costs include the following: computer equipment and software, copy machines and the monthly cost of maintaining them, monthly cell-phone costs, phone service and long-distance bills, Internet provider costs, proprietary system fees, and camera car costs. Another payout is the cost to build and maintain a professional website. You will have to pay monthly for hosting and yearly for your domain name. You will also have to pay bills for heat, electric, and maybe even a security system.

Some costs are easily forgotten when figuring the expenses of running an auto repossession business, but they add up quickly. Some of these expenses include printer paper, ink, office cleaning supplies and other business-related items that you will need to purchase. You will probably pay out for an IT professional to service your company, the cost of computer programs and antivirus programs, a snow removal service to plow, and a lawn-care business to maintain the grass.

As you can see, owning and operating your own repossession business can be costly. Before you take on this financial investment, I would advise you to figure out if it makes more sense financially to work for a company or start your own.

Utilizing Spotters to Reduce Fuel Costs, Mileage, and Wear and Tear

I know more than a few companies that utilize their camera cars not only to grid their service areas, but also to go out and spot addresses on repo assignments their company has issued. These companies basically have their wreckers sitting on standby until a camera-car driver calls them to make a pickup. By using this system, the only mileage put on the wrecker is directly to and from the address where the collateral was spotted and picked up. The wreckers only move when collateral is located. I even know of one company where the agents stay at their house during their shift while waiting to be called out. In these cases, the repo agent and the camera driver split 50/50 on what they are paid for the repo. The repo agent is actually being paid less per repo than most other companies pay their agent for a full repo, but they are also working less.

Maximize Your Profits
Through Multiple Streams of Income

You can maximize your profits and also add manpower and equipment to your business that will pay for itself. Your auto repossession work is one stream of income that is available to you. You are paid for voluntary and involuntary repossessions. You can also make money on storage fees and sometimes charge the client for making keys.

Some other areas in the business can also pump up your profits. I wanted to offer my clients a one-stop shopping experience by offering a wide variety of service to lenders. By doing this, you will reap the profits. Some repo companies only offer collateral recovery services, but I found many ways to use the equipment and manpower sitting idle to put additional cash in my pocket.

Utilize All of Your Equipment and Expertise

Take transport, for instance. Every repo company should have a transport division. A company can have a fleet of transport trailers and trucks or a fleet of rollbacks or a combination of both. The transport division can be picking up lease turn-ins at dealerships and transporting them to auction. They can be transporting repossessed collateral to the auctions, and while there, they can pick up and transport vehicles that were bought by used car dealerships. There is no need to go the auction loaded and then return empty—on half of the trip you are losing out on possible revenue.

Another way to make money is to offer skip tracing services under a different name that are operated in the same office as your repo company. You can do skip work on the accounts you are already working for your clients and also do skip work for them and other lenders through your skip tracing company. The two complement each other and help to pull in more profit. This profit is within your reach and ripe for the taking. Why should some skip company make the cash? Having your own skip company is simply one more way to boost your profit.

I can think of additional ways to amplify your business with the equipment that you have. Some companies do nothing but field visits. As a matter of fact, many lenders have a field visit done prior to issuing an account out for repo. Lenders will pay $100 or more for a field visit, and you should make sure that you are profiting from that aspect of the business. You could have an employee who is out spotting vehicles and also doing field visits. If you have a good database and record the result of the door knock, house description and any other pertinent information, then you can forward this information to your agent if he is issued the account. Once again, the lender does not need to know that you are the same company. Many times, different departments handle field visits and repossessions. All of the field visit information can be relayed via different proprietary work flow systems.

Even More Profit for Your Repossession Company

Another one of those ways is to have a rollback on call 24 hours a day for private towing. This service benefits your repo company by putting an extra man and an extra piece of equipment on the street at the company's disposal. Your driver can be doing private tows and service calls and, in the meantime, can be used to pick up vehicles from around the area that have been recovered by your repo agents. This addition saves the agents the time of traveling back and forth to your storage lot and also helps to lower the company fuel costs and wear and tear on your fleet.

The rollback can be available for tows, lockouts, transports, and the shuffling of collateral back to your shop. The other possibility is using the rollback to pick up vehicles that have been spotted by one of your employees who is driving around in a car looking for repos to pick up. I know of one repo agent who "steals" a car as quick in a rollback as most agents do in a self-loader. He sometimes prefers a rollback and picks up two cars at a time before returning to the storage yard.

Police Towing and Recovery

Another option for earning additional revenue is in the area of police towing. Big money can be earned by contracting with the police for towing and storage. Working with the police in the towing business is also a way to build a good working relationship with the department and build friendships with officers as well. If you can get on the police towing list, I would add police towing to the list of what your company does.

Repossession companies usually have towing equipment, so why not use the equipment that you have to increase your cash flow? If you operated a pizza restaurant, adding spaghetti, fettuccine, garlic bread and Caesar salads to your menu would not prove difficult. If you owned a shoe repair shop, I would not suggest that you sell 24 different flavors of ice cream. The two businesses are completely unrelated. But if you own a repossession company, you probably have drivers, tow trucks, rollbacks, car haulers, office staff, phones, cell phones, and a storage lot. All of this equipment should be put to use to add more dollars to your bank account.

TWO MORE STREAMS OF INCOME

How Big is Your Storage Lot?

If you have a large storage lot or extra space, you have another stream of income for your company. I know one repo company owner who allows semi drivers to park their rigs at the back of his property. Most of these drivers live in neighborhoods where no commercial trucks are allowed. They are not parking in the fenced-in storage area where the collateral is kept, but a different area entirely. This particular company owns a large property and rents out space to 15 to 20 truckers at a monthly fee of $100 each, bringing in $1500 to $2000 a month. I asked him if he had had any issues, and he said none at all. One added plus was having truckers coming and going on his property at all hours, which was another deterrent to possible theft and break-ins.

Key Cutting and Programming

Do you own key cutting and programming equipment? Dealerships charge a considerable fee to make program keys for businesses and for people. I did not do a great deal of work in the area of making and programming keys, but neither did I advertise that service. Without advertising, I would guess that I had 15 customers a month who paid me to make and program one or two keys for their vehicle. We charged less than a dealership, but the small amount of money that came in each month was enough to cover the payment on a new wrecker!

I have wondered if I had advertised this service and built it up to 60 customers a month, what I could have pulled in for the business. After all, sixty customers a month at only $60 per key would bring in an additional $3000 a month, which is an extra $36,000 a year.

I have heard a number of repossession company owners advise others not to add any of these services. I have even had a few of them make fun of me for the recommendations and suggestions I have made in this book. The ones who are against or make fun of offering any of these extra services usually own an average or unsuccessful repossession company. I have learned that these types of owners cannot think outside of the box. Sad to say, unless they start, they will never grow their business and will continue to live life being negative about everything.

CHAPTER FIFTEEN

"I just repossessed this bike, and you know what that means! A three-day road trip for us, baby!! Grab some drinks, and let's hit the road!!!"

Tips for Being Successful in the Repossession Business

My company maintained a superb reputation with all of my clients. I always shot straight with them, communicated with them, and never lied to them. If I made a mistake or one my employees did, I owned up to right away. In fact, I made the call before the client had to ask me about what went wrong.

Thousands of Dollars Found

One time I repossessed a vehicle from a bar that the debtor basically sat in getting drunk every day. He was unemployed and essentially homeless, spending his night passed out while couch surfing at his friend's houses. We pulled the collateral, brought it back to my shop, and began to inventory the property in the vehicle. I found several thousand dollars in an envelope under the seat.

The debtor was unemployed and had no place to live. I could have kept that cash, and the client would never have believed the debtor. What did I do? It was 3:00 a.m., but I called the client and left a message detailing the exact amount of cash that had been found and then locked it up in my office. Both the client and debtor were shocked. Guess what? That client would never in a million years have believed a debtor who accused me of theft of property in the future. I had plenty of other instances concerning found property with most of my other clients where I did exactly the same thing. My word with my client was as good as gold, and they knew I was honest and truthful.

Tickets for Running Toll Booths

We all like a nice Harley, high-end sports cars, and my favorite vehicle make—Bentleys! We picked up thousands of these types of vehicles. I loved to look at them, and I loved to dream about owning one someday. I think I sat on a few Harleys in my pole barn and sat behind the wheel of a couple of sports cars worth a couple of hundred thousand dollars.

As much as I loved those toys' being kept at my storage lot, I never took them out joyriding. I know of a few repossession companies where joyriding around town in a cool "ride" is a common practice. I know of one company that used hundreds of pieces of collateral to drive around spotting other collateral and door knocking accounts. This company enjoyed these "free" rides for years.

The company finally got caught when hundreds of debtors went to a major lender with proof that the repo company had been driving vehicles they had repossessed. The debtors knew because they had received hundreds of tickets in the mail for running toll booths weeks after their vehicles had been repossessed. You may not run a toll, but you might be involved in a major accident or pass a client on the road driving that Ferrari they had you pick up a few weeks ago. The price in the long run is not worth the risk. Don't give in to your desire to be cool or to have some fun; it will catch up with you eventually!

MY ROLLBACK NEEDS TIRES!

We received an order for a ratty old rollback that was owned by a local towing company that had gone out of business. When the rollback was turned over, we knew that it was going straight to the auction without any possibility of redemption. I was looking at that old truck and saw that it had brand-new tires all the way around it. I am talking tires with less than a hundred miles on them! The rollback was a piece of junk, but those tires were tire-shop-showroom shiny and new.

My rollback, sitting in my lot, was in great shape, other than the fact that I needed to replace every single tire on that truck. You guessed it! The very tires that I needed for my rollback were the exact same size tires on the rollback we had just repossessed. It was sitting in my storage lot, hidden from all eyes, and dusk was fast approaching.

Did I switch out those tires in the dark of night and send that junky rollback to the auction with my rollback's tires that needed replacing? They certainly matched the condition of the rollback. The client would never have known the difference. Not for one second did that exchange of tires cross my mind. That old rollback with the brand-new tires was delivered to auction that night. And the very next week, I dropped a bunch of money on new tires for my rollback. Did that expenditure hurt? Not one bit because acting with honesty and integrity never hurts!

Do right all of the time, and you will go far in the repossession business. Do not take advantage of your clients; be honest with them and treat them right. If you are thinking about or tempted to do something questionable, ask yourself, "Would I want the client to know about this action?"

Tip 1
Make Time for the Important Things

Family Time

None of us tough repo men like to talk about this subject, which definitely needs to be addressed because neglecting your family can result in an outcome that you will not like. We have all been there. You are sitting down to a family dinner or just about to watch your son pitch the most important game of the season and the phone rings. The car has been spotted, or one of the agents who works for you has got himself into a pickle. Whatever it is, you are expected to drop everything and handle business. These kinds of interruptions to family time can be quite hurtful and cause a great deal of tension with your loved ones.

Nothing is worth losing your family over—not one thing! No lender will ever break away from his daughter's swim meet to go and check on an account for you or take a call from you! So why should you? Repo agents have to balance work and family very carefully. I would suggest that if you have something important to do with your family, you should find one of your workers to cover emergencies.

In the repo business, you tend to have that mobile phone to your ear 24 hours a day. If you do not have the phone in your hand, then you most likely will have a repo order, a lockout tool, or a tow chain in your hand. If you are in the industry, you know it is true. You have to be disciplined enough to separate your work time from your family time.

This business can overtake your life and definitely lead to divorce court. The repo industry can cause your children to hate the business because you never have time for them. After all, when you are home, you are always on the phone talking about business. They do not want to hear you talking about the Hummer that you have to pick up; they want to have your full attention. Your family wants you to be interested in their lives too.

The repo business is a fast-paced business, and if you are slow, you will lose money. In order to continue to make money and have time for your family, I recommend that you live by some semblance of a schedule. Take an evening each week to spend with your wife or girlfriend as a special time together. I call it a date night. When you are out with her, turn off the phone and do not discuss business. If you can't stand the thought of shutting off your phone, then leave the phone on and set the ringer to silent.

Knowing who has called you will give you peace of mind until you can get back to them later. If you do not pull the phone out every time in vibrates, then your lady will never know. She will also think she is the most important concern in your life!

Take Your Kids Fishing

Every week set aside time for your children. Take your kids fishing for the day. Play sports with them and take them to get a bite to eat each week. Make sure you attend your children's athletic events and other activities. When you do take some time off, stay focused on your children and forget the repo business for a few hours. I promise it won't hurt; it will feel great!

If you are in the repo business, plan on working long hours and spending little time at home. If you are not careful, your absence will strain your relationship with your family, and they will resent the repo business. To avoid that, you need to have quality time with your family when you are at home. You should make them feel that they are so important, you will take a day off to be with them. Make the most of holidays and be sure to do something to make the day unforgettable. Remember your lady's birthday and always be there for your kids' birthdays as well.

I was always guilty of forgetting birthdays and other special events, and I can promise you that I paid dearly for my negligence. At the end of the day, we all have to keep the way we live life in perspective. Is your business important? Of course it is, and so is making money. You can't live without making money. However, if you become rich because your repo business is highly successful and you lose your family over it, then none of the blood, sweat, and tears you put into the business will be worth it. Work hard, make money, but do not forget to enjoy life with your family.

Tip 2
Be Positive All of the Time

I am no Anthony Robbins, but I am a fairly optimistic person. I believe one of the biggest problems found in the auto repossession business is negativity. From the owner to the office staff to the repossession agent working the streets, a constant "doom-and-gloom" attitude pervades the business. When you go to work tomorrow, simply take a look around your office. Is your office staff looking depressed and complaining? Are your agents moaning and groaning about dead accounts and bad paper that they have in their folders?

The auto repossession industry has a cloud of negativity surrounding it at all times, so why add to it by having a negative attitude? I heard the "bad news" every day when I owned my company. Agents would get new paper and prejudge the account before ever running it. They were absolutely sure that "The car won't be there," "The debtor has moved to another state," "This is a junk order," or "This particular lender always issues bad paper."

Auto repossession agents seem to believe they have some sort of mystical powers that allow them to look at a phone number, an address, or just a debtor's name on an order and be able to predict the status of said vehicle! How could they know that by looking at a new order for 30 seconds? That approach is nothing more than displaying a negative attitude. Having that type of mindset will be reflected in the agent's ability to be a successful repossessor. They will pick up fewer cars, face more confrontations with debtors and definitely make both you and them a lot less money!

Optimistic Thinking = Big Profits
How can a person maintain a positive attitude in a business

full of heartache and bad news? Being positive when you work in an industry where you are taking a person's vehicle from them can be tough, but we can be positive about ourselves and our professional job performance. We can look at each order with the attitude, "I am going to pick up this car on the first run." An agent can plan ahead in his mind how the recovery will take place perfectly without any issues. He can have a positive mindset that he will pick up the vehicle without damaging it or having a violent confrontation with the debtor. The agent can prepare himself with what to say to the debtor or to calm him down if he happens to come out of the house during the recovery process.

Agents can treat people with decency and not further escalate the situation by using negative words or actions. The scenario is already unfavorable, but professional auto repossession agents should have the ability to control the situation. This is done by planning ahead for the outcome to be a positive one. The agent needs to be sure that he is familiar with the information on the repossession order, so if the debtor confronts him, he can put him at ease. He should be able to calmly explain to him that he has to repossess the collateral and then provide him with the lender's contact information, the collector's first name and extension number, and the amount past due—if that information was provided. Staying positive, being informed about your accounts and remaining calm is the key to having a successful night of repossessing cars.

Tip 3

Get At Least One New Client Every Month

Some auto repossession company owners will never get a *yes* or a *no* about new business because they do not take the time to pick up the phone to call any potential lender clients. I realize the repo businesses are always busy repossessing cars, making keys, dealing with debtors' property, talking on the phone with their current clients, and managing their employees. If you own an auto repossession business, I am sure you can add a thousand more reasons for being so busy!

However, if you are not consistently building your lender client list, then you will eventually lose ground. In the future, one or more lenders will stop using your repossession services, regardless of the wonderful service you are providing them. I have talked to countless auto repo company owners who have lost clients for whom they did work for many years. These clients loved them, and they enjoyed long-lasting relationships with them. However, one day they lost them as clients due to mergers, a collection manager's retiring, the lender's making the decision to go the forwarder route or some other reason.

I know of one owner who saw his best client vanish when a bank president's son decided to go into the collateral recovery industry. When I had my repo company, I received calls every week from lenders looking to give me business. I was making good money and had more than enough work, and I could have sat back and just taken the new work when I got those calls. Fortunately, I knew that a business that was not growing was dying. I made it a point to sign on new lenders every month—even if I only added one. How did I do that? I decided to call a certain number of potential lender clients every day. Some of the calls I made were first-time calls, and others were follow-up calls to the lenders I had called previously.

Set yourself a goal to call and TALK to five possible clients every day. I capitalized TALK because leaving five voicemails does not count. Dial clients until you have spoken with five and are able to get them your company packet either by email, fax or snail mail.

If a lender declines your services, tell the person with whom you are talking that you would like to check back with them in a month or at another time they agree to. Also get their name, direct line (if they have one), an email address, and a fax number. Anyone who has been in this business for any length of time will tell you about a time they spoke with a collection manager who seemed interested in using them, but they were never able to get them back on the phone again. So develop multiple ways to stay in contact with them!

Your services will be declined by many, but don't let that stop you from contacting them again in the future with a follow-up call. As your "no" list grows, keep making your five fresh calls a week and add one-to-three follow-up calls to your routine.

I keep hearing owners telling me that they do not have time to make sales calls. If you are thinking that too, then you need to make a commitment right now to make time to grow your business. I have been in the repo business, and besides working hard, I spent a fair amount of time horseplaying with my agents and staff, drinking coffee, taking extra-long lunches, visiting with friends, and even watching television in my office. I had a plethora of good times running my company, but I had to prioritize my time. We can always find time for the things we enjoy doing. I enjoyed being successful and making money, so I made time to make that happen. Do not get discouraged when you are making your sales calls. Remember, each "no" is one step closer to your goal!

Tip 4
The Motivation of the Word No

How can the word *no* motivate you to build a successful auto repossession business? If you are going to be an entrepreneur, you will frequently hear the dreaded *no* word. The first *no* you will hear is when you ask the people you know if they think it is a good idea to get into the auto repo business.

I remember when I was thinking of buying the repossession company for which I was working. I asked some people in my life if they thought it would be a good idea. Ninety-nine percent of the people I asked told me "No!"

If you are going to succeed as a repossessor, you need to take the word *no* as a personal challenge. When I was told, "No, it is a bad business move," I thought to myself *Really? Watch me!* I bought the company, and I succeeded!

From day one, you need to get into the mindset that a *no* CANNOT stop you. In the repo business, be prepared to hear the word *no* a few more times and plan your reaction. You will hear *no* when you seek business financing. You will hear *no* when you apply for a loan for a wrecker. You might hear *no* a few times when you try to secure auto repossession insurance. You will hear *no* a hundred times or more when you try to sign up clients. Experiencing *no* so many times will be some great training for you! Debtors will tell you *no* day in and day out when you try to get them to turn over their collateral! You will need to be able to conquer the word *no*! You need to resolve this issue in your mind if you want to be the owner of a successful auto repossession business.

When you hear the word *no*, you have a decision about how to interpret its meaning. If you are told, "You can't do that," you can take that in and believe it and say to yourself, "You're right; I can't." Every conversation has a buyer and a seller. If you are "selling" me that I can't do it and I "buy" it, then I can't do it.

On the other hand, for me, I would take your telling me I can't do something and turn that doubt into racing fuel. Hearing that *no* fuels me and challenges me to conquer the *no*. Hearing that *no* is actually a positive motivation for me and, as a business owner, you need to have that spirit as part of your makeup.

You will need to make a change within yourself if that is not one of your attributes. One way to change is to look at the people who are telling you, "No, it is not a good idea." How successful are they? Is their life the kind of life you would be delighted to emulate? Do not take advice from someone who has never done anything! If you talk to some of the auto repossession industry "greats" who are truly successful, they will rarely tell you that you can't do it. The failures in life are always the ones who will tell you that you cannot do it.

I talk to auto repossession company owners every day. One

attribute is very different among the successful ones than among the ones who are barely making it. That attribute does not involve cash flow, under-funding, not having enough trucks, employee problems, or a lack of clients. That attribute involves hearing the word *no* and the reaction to that word. Learn to positively react to the word *no* and turn that negative into fuel that will drive you to reach your goals. If you do, NOTHING can stop you from having a successful auto repossession business.

Tip 5
Just say *No*!

The previous tip addressed learning to respond to the word *no* and how to be persistent in this business. This tip was inspired by a friend who owns a very successful repossession agency. He has another thought about the word *no*—but in a different way. You should not only learn how to overcome the obstacle word *no*, but you need to learn how to say *no* as well. Saying *no* could be used in response to a request for free storage or perhaps for doing work on a contingency basis or possibly for a low fee for repossession work.

Far too many auto repossession companies are taking any business they can get without weighing the costs. These "eager beavers" are jumping at any work that is thrown at them are the reason why auto finance companies are expecting every contractor to work for cheap rates and provide free services. These same lenders are in the business of making money and yet expect you to work for fees that cause you to lose money. They would not be providing auto loans to people if they were not making money, and you should not work for them if you are not making money.

When I talk to people in the auto finance world, I often ask them a couple of questions that make them squirm. The first question is: "Would you do your job if you were only going to get paid if the people paid or the car gets recovered?" Another question is, "Would you come in to work on Saturday and Sunday if you were not going to get paid for those hours?" None of them ever say that they would and then I compare that to freebies that auto repossession company owners are often asked to do by clients.

About ten years ago, I did work for a client who paid well. We received $325 a car, plus keys, plus transport with a cure fee—if we persuaded the debtor to pay up. We picked up about 100 or more voluntary repos a month that made it a guaranteed $50,000-a-month account for us. Obviously, we were very happy to do their auto repossession work because we were making a nice profit.

I recently spoke with an auto repossession company owner in my former area who is currently doing the same company's work. He is doing their involuntary repossessions for a whopping, all-inclusive fee of $285 a car. He must make keys, transport the cars to auction, and does not receive a cure fee for that price. I know he is not making money, he knows he is not making money, and you know it too. He should have said, "No" to that account from the start. The cost of running a repossession business has gone up since I did auto repo work for them.

How is it possible that this lender's fee has gone down and not risen to $450 per repo plus keys and transport with a cure?

That question demands an answer, and the answer is that some poor soul needed work so badly that he was afraid to say "No!" Lenders weigh the decision on whether or not to put you on their vendor list, and you need to do the same when thinking about doing work for a client. If you will not make money working for a client, then you need to just say "No."

I am not talking about making a living either! A person makes a living at a job, but business owners need to make a healthy profit! Weigh the costs before bringing on a new client, and if you are not going to make good money, then you need to turn them down with a confident "No!"

TIP 6
AVOID BURNOUT

Over the last couple of decades, I have seen auto repossession companies come and go. Both friends in the business and competitors have closed their doors for a variety of reasons. Some closed their doors due to money management and poor business practices. Others closed their doors as a result of illness or old age. I have often heard divorce and personal problems cited as reasons for throwing in the towel.

Out of all the reasons I have heard, I would say one of the most frequent reasons for closing an auto repossession business was just plain being tired and giving up. Time and time again, I have had repo company owners tell me they were burned out and closing their doors. They were tired of battling with staff, clients, debtors, and the other headaches that come with owning an auto repossession. If you, as the owner, are burned out, your business will also become burned out. Your office staff and repossession agents will catch vibes you put off, become burned out too, and business will suffer.

Never let your employees see you down. For your sake and your business' sake, you need to always be on top side. Having a positive attitude will be contagious and will lead to your business running better. Of course, this attitude will lead to higher profits and business growth.

I have been in the offices of both types of companies—the "burned-out" one and the "on-topside" one. The two are farther apart than the East Coast is from the West Coast, and the "on-topside" business is the one raking in the cash. Not only is the business making money, but the staff and owner are having a blast doing what they love! In the "burned-out" office, the thick tension in the air can be sliced and diced. The pain can be seen in everyone's face, and a knowledgeable business person can almost predict the date and time they will go bankrupt.

Most of us got into this business with a great love for the auto repossession industry and the life that goes with the business. If you get burned out, you will lose the love for this industry, and just like a marriage, the relationship will come to a painful end. Feeling burnout coming on? Spend some time with your family or get involved in a charity!

Tip 7
Repossessions and Collateral Damage
Accidents Happen

Repo agents often deal with volatile situations that put an

enormous amount of stress on them. There are times when they are snatching a car from a tight space. Many times agents are driving at night, sharing the road with both sleepy drivers and drunken drivers, and having their sight hindered by the darkness. If you plan to be in the repossessing business, then you must come to terms with the fact that accidents will happen. Collateral will be damaged. It may be someone or something else's fault, or it may be that one of your employees was at fault. When collateral in your possession is damaged, you need to be calm and assess the situation.

If an agent in the field is in an accident while driving or towing, he needs to contact the proper authorities and document what happened. Then you need to decide if you will turn the accident in to your insurance company or pay out of pocket for the damage. When I owned my company, we had very few accidents. In fact, I can only think of two at the moment. I had a high deductible to keep my insurance costs down and, to the best of my knowledge, we never had an insurance claim.

Some companies decide that they will not tell the finance company about an accident. This cover-up can be a dreadful mistake and cost the company dearly. Many companies have lost their largest account over trying to cover-up damage they had caused to a vehicle they had repossessed. Fresh damage, which is often noticed by lenders, can raise questions. You never know when the debtor will redeem his vehicle and find that your agent had rammed his wheel lift into the front bumper of his car. You can argue that the damage was already there and show that it was noted on your condition report. You may even get by with the dishonesty, but your client will always have a doubt in his mind as to how honest you are. Lenders know that accidents do happen, and they usually can accept it and also appreciate your honesty. If you are honest about an accident and take care of the necessary repairs, then you are establishing a track record with your client. When someone makes a false claim that you damaged his vehicle, then the client will remember that you have no problem admitting when you are at fault.

Honesty and Integrity

One time one of my drivers was towing a car out of a driveway. The wheels were slightly cocked, and the steering wheel was locked. In trying to get the car away from the house, the agent damaged the front fender and headlight. He was my best agent and had been with me for years, so I was not even the least bit upset. I was, however, terrified to call our largest client and tell the account manager that we had damaged their collateral.

I had the weekend to think about how to handle the incident, and I had several people advise me not to mention the damage unless the debtor redeemed the car. I simply could not bring myself to follow their advice.

The first thing Monday morning I was on the phone to the rep at the finance company. I told her that we had secured her collateral but that there had been a problem. She did not even react when I told her we had damaged the vehicle and was quite happy when I told her that I would have the car repaired.

She told me that the debtor was not redeeming the vehicle,

and for that reason she was very surprised that I had been honest about the accident. She added, "The collections manager just had a training class for all of the reps in my department. During the class he discussed damage occurring to collateral during the execution of repossession. Repossession companies always lie about damage they have done. On top of that, they never take responsibility for the repairs."

I couldn't figure out why she was telling me about this training class. She continued, "I am going straight to his office to tell him that your company *is* different."

I saw a big increase in business from that client because I told the truth. Honesty can do nothing but build strong relationships with your clients.

TIP 8
DON'T FEAR TECHNOLOGY OR NEW THINGS.

When I got into repossessions, no proprietary systems were in place. We received orders via a fax machine and sent the condition report back the same way. There were no programmable keys or airbags, so we dent pulled ignitions, used a screwdriver to start a car, and popped a new ignition in when we returned to the storage yard. There were no camera cars, no Clearplan—nothing! Just you, the moon, and your repo tools.

I know some repo company owners who won't change with the times. A few of them with whom I interact still have their orders faxed, carry no computer in their truck, use no LPR cameras or any other cutting-edge technology that is available to repossessors today.

In the repossession industry, you have to mold yourself and your company to the latest technology and tools that are available. If you don't stay current, you will lose and miss out on so much business. So toss those paper city maps in the incinerator and start using GPS. Add everything else that is out there that will make your job easier and bring in more money for your company!

Tip 9
Give Back to the Community;
Donate to Worthy Causes

I can't possibly neglect the area of giving when it comes to building a successful repossession company. I truly believe the statements "what goes around comes around" and "you reap what you sow." If you are a dirty player and always out to hurt people, you will be paid back someday. Those paybacks can really hurt.

Being a business owner is a big responsibility in more ways than one. Sure, it is difficult to manage employees, keep your trucks running, keep the clients happy, make sure the bills are being paid, and grow a business. All of that is a part of being a business owner.

One easily forgotten part of owning a business is our responsibility to the community in which we live and work. We have a responsibility not only to take but also to give back. Many social programs, nonprofit companies, and churches are desperately in need of people who care enough to help. You can invest in your community and the people who live there in many ways. You are already investing by providing jobs for people who live in the community. Your employees have to work and get the job done in order to receive a paycheck, but I am not talking about that aspect. Rather, I am addressing the matter of freely giving without expecting anything in return.

Your choice could be Toys for Tots, a local domestic violence shelter, a church that is holding a vacation Bible school for children, or helping out at a pancake breakfast that the fire or police department is hosting. Everyone knows that repossession companies have loads of unclaimed property. These items can be donated to the Salvation Army, or you could have a company rummage sale and donate the proceeds to your favorite charity or church. Oftentimes, community beautification projects need workers as well as money.

Rewards That Come with Giving

Most donations are tax-deductible and are also excellent ways of making contacts and helping your business to grow. I built a rather large and successful repossession company that grew from a tiny company operating on a shoestring budget to a powerhouse repo company with a great deal of equipment, a large workload, and big profits. I made a lot of money and accomplished many great things with the repo business I used to own. I was able to sell it to a large corporation and retire before I was 40 years old.

I can testify that this success was the result of a plethora of hard work, many long hours, good business strategy, hiring the right people, choosing the right equipment, and a whole lot of luck. However, I wholeheartedly believe that the number-one reason I was successful was that I gave back to my community. I donated time and money to local FOPs, gave to my local church, bought groceries for needy families, and gave to many other worthy projects.

We were also never out to gouge anyone with my towing or service prices. Often we did free or at cost tows for people who I knew did not have the money to pay the going rate. I can honestly say that I was never out to hurt anyone, and I sleep well at night knowing that.

There are more worthy causes in your community than you can possibly imagine. Look around and talk to some of your city's leaders; you can easily find out where the needs are. Besides the tax write-offs and the business contacts you make, nothing is more satisfying than doing for others and not expecting one thing in return. The rewards for these deeds will be far greater than the ones where we are expecting something for what we do.

Tip 10
Do Unto Others as You Would Have Them Do to You

Think Before You Hurt Someone

Treat everyone—from your employees to your clients to the debtor to the people in your community—with respect. Think of the times when you were treated poorly and how badly the treatment made you feel about yourself. Remember how their lack of respect hurt you and how the mistreatment made you feel about the people who wronged you. Take note as to how you still view them and how you probably view these people in a negative light.

Don't be that person who hurts others so badly that they will never forget you or the hurt you inflicted. You may only have one chance to impact a person's life. Do you want it to be in a positive way or a negative way? I can assure you that being positive is the more fulfilling of the two!

Problems

We all have problems—maybe not the same problems, but problems. People are hurting all around us and may be experiencing the worst days of their life. You do not know their circumstances or what bad news they just received. Be sympathetic and empathetic toward people. You do not know how bad things are for them.

Make a Difference

All the money in the world and all the successes business brings are still not the greatest rewards. I have always said that I want to live my life, knowing I made a difference in the lives of as many people as I possibly can. You cannot appropriate their hurts or circumstances, but you change someone's life for a brief moment—perhaps through a smile, a kind word, a helping hand or simply treating the person like a human being.

CHAPTER SIXTEEN

"Cheapo Repo Co. offered me a job when I get to work release! I'm experienced at stealing cars. I just did eight years for auto theft!"

IN CLOSING

THIS CHAPTER WILL probably be the shortest one of the book. As I come to a close, I ask that you all help with one matter. Let's all work together to make the repossession industry better. By working together, the business will become stronger. Eliminating the "good-ol'-boys'-club" image is a necessity for the industry's betterment. Instead, may we strive together to make the industry an all-inclusive club for those who will rise to the occasion with standards and professionalism.

How can we make the industry better and stronger? We need to work *together*, rather than working *against* one another. Stop the backbiting, the gossip, bashing one another and throwing each other under the bus. There is an abundance of repossession work to go around! Instead, lend a helping hand to one another rather than being a hateful competitor in business. Set some common goals to improve and standardize the industry through training and mentoring.

The repossession industry needs to adopt the age-old motto of "United we stand, divided we fall" to inspire some unity, partnership, and collaboration within their ranks. Instead of hiring and firing the same agents and recycling them to your competitors, hire some new blood! The industry needs to stop hiring thugs, criminals and scammers! Instead, through career development, train up a team of agents who will take great pride in their craft. Train them and mentor them into becoming professional repossessors who see the big picture. Train them to recognize that a career can be had in this business.

THE BENEFITS OF BEING PROFESSIONAL

The more professionalized this industry is, the more owners can charge for their services. I honestly believe that many clients would pay more if the repossession set the bar way higher than it currently is. Not only would it bring in higher fees, but it would also bring the owner more repossession accounts. Certainly, the clients will want to reward the best of the best this industry has to offer. It will definitely save owners money in repairs, lawsuits, and other business costs.

Have you ever wondered why auto repossession insurance is so expensive? Why wouldn't it be? An unregulated industry is being insured that is not only unwilling to regulate itself, but also enjoys living that way! What training is in place in the repo industry? Every other occupation and field touts its training and standards. Perhaps the industry as a whole could negotiate a discount on repossession insurance if high quality education across the board were a standard requirement.

This teaching would include more than repossession laws and compliance; safety training for repossession agents, sexual harassment, and other training that every industry mandates would be included. How about something as simple as training in cultural diversity?

Recently I was at a repo company and witnessed a few

employees making racial slurs about other employees and debtors. If that egregious attitude does not scream the need for training, I do not know what does!

CHANGING THE REPOSSESSION INDUSTRY MINDSET

Through the years, I have had many conversations with repossession company owners, repo agents, collection managers, account representatives and even general counsels of various creditors. What role the person to whom I am talking plays in the repossession industry does not seem to matter when it comes to the one common denominator I have found across the board in this industry. Everyone is getting the industry wrong in one way or another.

Many misconceptions, so much misinformation, and an abundance of mistrust exists in this business. A civil line of communication needs to be open between repossession company owners, repo agents, collection managers, account representatives, and various creditors; the dialogue needs to be ongoing. An open-minded meeting of the minds needs to occur so everyone can better understand what the other person is encountering.

HOW IS EACH ONE GETTING IT WRONG?

I want to address the traits I see in the front-line repossession agent first. Many repo agents are negative about everything. Hearing them constantly complain that all of the repossession assignments they are assigned are junk orders or maybe the accounts of "this forwarder" or "that lender" are the worst to manage is standard behavior. Many of them think they know everything about the repo industry, and no one can teach them anything about the business.

If the repo company owner can persuade the agents who work for him to be more positive, then the industry would be a whole lot better. Being positive creates a healthier work environment, and studies prove being positive can greatly increase productivity. If you hear them complaining about a client, try to point out that client's positives. When you hear them engaging in negative talk, do not join in; rather, spin the conversation in a positive way. There is always a bright side to every situation.

As the owner, make sure that you encourage your agents. Treat them well, care about them, and always be there when they need you. Invest your time in your agents' career development and make sure you are constantly mentoring and training them. I have watched plenty of owners treat their agents like dirt. Treating employees badly will never build a team of great agents in your company, and making that mistake will definitely hurt your profits.

Your goal as an owner should be to have a healthy work environment for your staff, to experience a low employee turnover rate, and to focus on making your team better all the time. Your company would certainly operate more smoothly if you employed a group of great agents who stayed working for you for a very long time.

THE REPOSSESSION COMPANY OWNERS

This group can also be extremely negative about the industry. Leading by example is the best model, and if the owners are negative, expect their staff to be negative. Often, an owner can end up not being hands on and rarely working in the field. The repossession industry is always changing, and as an owner, you need to keep you finger on the pulse of the field in which you are working. To do that, you need to get out there as often as you can and work with your agents. By doing so, you can identify their strengths and weaknesses, focus on fixing what needs to be fixed, and keeping them doing that which they are already doing well.

Another area where many owners appear to be deficient is in communicating with the clients. An owner needs to maintain an open dialogue with his clients so he will know the challenges being faced in the field. Every owner's desire and goal should be to assist his clients with any difficulty.

The average auto finance employee from account rep to the collection manager to the role of general counsel has no idea what agents and repo company owners experience daily. Educating employees on what occurs on the owner's end when it is appropriate to do so is up to the owner. He should not instruct in a condescending, overbearing, or insulting way; rather, he should calmly and effectively communicate with them so they can understand his side of the industry.

You may be wondering if I will address where the collection managers, account representatives and general counsels of various creditors are getting it wrong. Nope. I am starting where my heart lies—with the industry that I love. I believe correcting ourselves on this side of the industry is far more constructive. Let them handle fixing their end. I can promise that if we do better on our end of the industry, every other area of the industry will be forced to rise to the occasion and better themselves too. It may not happen today or tomorrow, but in time that will be the end result. I am confident of that.

In closing, let me wish you all the best in this industry. I pray that you will stay safe and that you will prosper personally, spiritually, and financially. I firmly believe that this industry is one of the best businesses to be in. I also believe that it might well be the last small business out there where wealth and success can still be found.

I have heard it said many times that no repossession company owner would want his son or daughter to be in this industry. "I want them to be a doctor or a lawyer!" or so they say. I end with this: is the repo industry in such bad shape that you would not want to build your business so you could pass it on to your next generation? If the answer is yes, then I must ask you, "What on earth are you going to do to fix it?"

Appendix 1

Nationwide Skip Tracing Websites

411.com — free people, phone, business and address searches

Amazon — Find someone's wish list.

Beacon — 16.5 million property records that are routinely updated, usually daily, from each jurisdiction's source data systems from over 500 local government organizations

Dun & Bradstreet — Often referred to as D&B, the company's database contains more than 265 million worldwide business records.

Facebook Search Tool — Find Facebook accounts by name, email screen name, and phone.

Federal Firearms License Search — The purpose of this program is to allow an FFL or other user to verify that a Federal Firearms License (FFL) is valid.

GSA Staff Directory Database — All GSA employees and contractors who are assigned to GSA are listed.

Instagram Search Tool

MySpace — Still used by some people, supposedly 1 billion active and inactive members, so it might be worth the search

LinkedIn — The world's largest professional network with more than 500 million users in more than 200 countries and territories worldwide

Lookup-ID.com — Facebook-supported searches for the following types: people, pages, places, check-ins, and more.

Melisa Data — multiple free- and fee-based searches

Multi Website Search Tool

Open Secrets — political contribution website

Peekyou — Collects and combines scattered content from social sites, news sources, homepages, and blog platforms to present comprehensive online identities; PeekYou brings a new perspective to people search.

People Finder — people, reverse phone, reverse address, zip code, and area code searches. Unlimited is $29.95 per month.

PPS Visualizer — converts GPS coordinates to an address or an address to GPS coordinates.

Skype — With over 600 million users, get a free account to search for Skype users. Your skip might be one of them.

Spy Dialer — A free people search that discreetly dials and allows you to listen to someone's cell phone voicemail so you know who you are calling; the spy dialer number shows on their phone as a missed call. Reverse phone look up and phone photo lookup that checks their number to their social media account for their photo.

TinEye — image search and recognition company.

Twitter Multi-Search Tool

United States Patent and Trademark Office — Using TTAB-VUE, you can view a TTAB proceeding file by entering the proceeding number, or search for proceedings by application number, registration number, mark, party, correspondent.

User Search — Searches for the person behind a username, email address, or phone number

Whoisology — A domain name ownership archive with literally billions of searchable and cross-referenced domain name "whois" records.

You Got the News — Alledgedly the #1 search engine for US News; search 5,000+ national, business, and local news sources

Zaba Search — search people, reverse phone numbers

Appendix 2

Glossary
of Repossession Terms

You will hear a plethora of words used in the auto repossession industry. Some you will hear every day; some you will only hear once, but it is important to know what they mean so you do not appear unprofessional. The following list contains some auto repossession terms and their definitions, as well as some abbreviations and their meanings.

Adjuster

An old-school term that means "repossessor."

Charge off

A declaration by a creditor that a debt is unlikely to be collected. A *charge off* is usually made on accounts over six months in arrears.

Collateral

Assets pledged by a borrower to secure a loan or other credit and subject to seizure in the event of default.

COLLECTIONS MANAGER

Oversees the activities of employees engaged in issuing repossessing orders to adjusters and generally is the individual who decides which repossession companies are on the lender's vendor list.

COLLECTOR

The employee of a lender that assigns, updates, and oversees accounts that are in the repossession stage of collections.

CONDITION REPORT

A detailed report on the condition of a vehicle's exterior and interior.

DEBTOR

The person who is responsible for the loan contract because he put his signature on it. A debtor may also be called a buyer or a maker. A second signer on a loan can be referred to as a co-debtor, co-maker and a co-buyer.

DOOR KNOCK

A door knock is when the repossessor makes contact with a debtor by knocking on the door to find out where the collateral is located.

FIELD VISIT

This is when an adjuster goes to a debtor's home, completes a vehicle condition report, and usually takes some digital photographs for the lender.

LIGHT SKIP

The process whereby a skip tracer or a collections rep performs a simple verification of the information a lender has on a debtor. This verifying is usually done via the Internet, by phone, by pulling a credit report, or by using a commercial data service to verify debtor information.

LIQUIDATION

The sale of collateral

PAPER

Simply put, a repo order. There can be *bad* paper or *junk* paper, which means the order does not list any accurate information. *Good* paper is when the repo order contains accurate information on the debtor and the location of the collateral. *Recycled* paper is an auto repossession order that has been sent to one repossession company that could not locate the collateral; the contact has then been sent to several repo agencies to continue the search with negative results.

PHONE BREAK

The act of identifying the owner of a phone number and the address the phone service is registered to.

QUALIFYING A VEHICLE

Oftentimes a transporter will use this phrase when trying to confirm if a vehicle is ready for transport.

REDEMPTION

A debtor has paid his loan current and will get his vehicle back.

REPLEVIN

A court action to recover possession of collateral.

SKIP

A person who has skipped out on his loan.

SKIP TRACER

A person who performs the task of locating a person's whereabouts.

STRAW PURCHASE

When a borrower finances a vehicle for a third party who usually has a bad credit rating. Lenders hate this practice and normally call the loan immediately.

TRAP LINE

A telephone service that "traps" the originating phone number of an incoming call, regardless of whether or not the caller I.D. is utilized. If a skip tracer knows someone who knows a skip, he will try to get a message passed to the skip, hoping he will call the trapline.

AUTO REPOSSESSION INDUSTRY SHORTHAND

Some auto repossession abbreviations you will likely come across in your repoman career are as follows. Don't embarrass yourself by having to call a lender to ask for the meaning.

Addy — address

Att G — attached garage

Det G — detached garage

DK — door knock

DNE — does not exist

GAR — garage

Invol — involuntary repossession

KaD — (or KAD) Knock and Demand; **knock**ing on the debtor's door to **demand** the collateral.

LM — left message

NLE — no longer employed

NUF — no unit found

POE — place of employment

Repo — repossession

ROC — return of collateral

TT — talk to

TTN — talk to neighbor

TX — phone number

UNV — unit not visible

VNV — vehicle not visible

VM — voice mail

Vol — voluntary repossession

APPENDIX 3

OTHER USEFUL INFORMATION

ASSOCIATIONS

Allied Finance Adjusters
3 Park Lane Ste 321
Douglassville, PA 19518
Phone: 800-843-1232
Fax: 888-949-8520
alliedfinanceadjusters.com
alliedfinanceadjusters@gmail.com

American Recovery Association
1400 Corporate Drive, Suite 175
Irving, Texas 75038
Phone: 972-755-4755
repo.org

Time Finance Adjusters
timefinanceadjusters.com/
1-800-874-0510
nicki@tfaguide.com – President
patrick@tfaguide.com – CEO

---

todd@tfaguide.com – V.P. Membership Chairman
william@tfaguide.com – Administrator

LPR COMPANIES

DRN
4150 International Plaza, Suite 800
Fort Worth, TX 76109-4875
Phone: 817-877-0077

MVTRAC
260 East Helen Road
Palatine, IL 60067
Main Office: 847-485-2300
Fax: 847-789-8819

REPOSSESSION INSURANCE

GLB Insurance Group of Nevada
Michael Mitchell
Phone: 702-768-1137
repoinsurance@gmail.com

American Transportation Insurance Group (ATIG)
Phone: 407-472-9600
Fax: 407-472-9605

Cagley & Associates Insurance Services
Phone: 805-338-7991
Fax: 805-418-7146

RSIG
Phone: 800-997-7224

Austin Insurance Inc.
Phone: 270-444-6818
Fax: 270-444-6809

Ken Cagley Insurance
Phone: 895-338-7992

Transportation Resources
Phone: 877-544-0705
Fax: 561-244-2507

Harding Brooks Insurance
Phone: 315-214-5822
Fax: 607-798-6693

Hatch Insurance Agency, Inc.
Phone: 602-995-5692
Fax: 602-995-5693

WCI — Walt Cagley Insurance
Phone: 805-497-2141

Brennan & Associates Insurance Services
Phone: 877-442-0096

Evolution Insurance Brokers
Phone: 801-304-5500

Hessler Insurance Solutions
Phone: 909-337-9437

REPOSSESSION SOFTWARE

RDN

620 S. Stapley Dr.
Suite 232
Mesa, AZ 85204
Support Phone: 817-204-0298
Recovery Companies: Option 1
Forwarder or Lender: Option 2
Fax: 602-412-5416

Recovery Manager Pro

Phone: 386-676-9817

Baja Recovery Software

Phone: 540-602-9690

Irepo

Phone: 602-864-7847

Repo Systems

Phone: 972-501-0375

RepoXR

Phone: 307-363-2886
Fax: 360-363-2883

WEBSITES FOR SKIP TRACING

TLO

tlo.com/

TLO's services include:

- Skip Tracing

- Investigate and analyze asset ownership and hidden assets.

- Locate and analyze people, places, businesses, and interrelationships over time

- Research criminal histories and associations

Accurint

1-866-809-9602

accurint.com/

Now owned by LexisNexis. Accurint is a widely accepted locate-and-research tool available to government, law enforcement, and commercial customers. Its proprietary data-linking technology returns search results in seconds to the user's desktop.

Accurint services include:

- **People Search** locates neighbors, associates, and possible relatives

- **Phones Plus** tracks down phone numbers not typically available to increase your chances of finding your subject. Access over 50,000,000 non-directory assistance records, including cell phone numbers

- **People at Work** links more than 132 million individuals to businesses and includes information such as business addresses, phone numbers, and possible dates of employment. Links individuals with businesses, addresses, relatives and vehicles

- **Advanced Person Search** helps find individuals when only old or fragmented data is available

- **Business Search** allows you to learn about companies before doing business with them by performing a comprehensive search on the corporation. Determine if they have filed for bankruptcy, who has liens against their assets, and if they are a legally operating company.

Belles Link

Phone: 970-670-4167

Quickly and easily search names, property records, phone numbers, addresses, and more. A flat-rate monthly fee for database searches means you never have to budget your skip tracing.

IRBfocus

2341-A Hansen Court

Tallahassee, FL 32301

Phone: 800-447-2112

Fax: 850-656-1738

irbsearch.com

IRBfocus gives you access to more than forty individual searches and reports to find the information you need. Each search fits under six main categories: people, assets, businesses, courts, licenses, and phones. Find out more about individual searches and reports below. Coverage for their information stretches across fifty states and all US territories. Within IRBfocus, each search and report displays a coverage map detailing the information provided. All search and report results are saved for seven days and are exportable as a PDF, Word Document, or Excel Spreadsheet.

Locate Plus

locateplus.com/

Phone: 888-746-3463

Locate Plus skip tracing software contains billions of current and historical cross-referenced public records to ensure your search is done right the first time. LocatePLUS serves investigators, legal, process servers, bail bondsmen, recovery, collections, finance, security, government and law enforcement to ensure they can locate anyone, anywhere. The proprietary investigative database cross-references billions of records to deliver search results in near-real-time.

WRECKER MANUFACTURERS

Detroit Wrecker Sales

Phone: 313-835-8700

Fax: 313-835-4838

DG Tow — Dynamic

Manhattan, New York, United States

Phone: 646-302-3535

Minute Man

Jenison, Michigan, United States

Phone: 877-593-6959

CHAPTER TITLE

———